HERO & FRIEND
My Days with Pistol Pete Maravich

Darrel Campbell

PERCUSSION

HERO & FRIEND

My Days with Pistol Pete Maravich
by
Darrel Campbell

Published by
Percussion Films, llc
Copyright © Darrel Campbell, 2019

ISBN-13: 978-0-578-21343-9

Cover design by Jeffrey Mardis

Printed in the United States of America

PUBLISHER'S NOTE:
While the author has made every effort to provide accurate telephone numbers, Internet addresses and other contact information at the time of publication, neither the publisher nor the author assumes any responsibility for errors, or for changes that occur after publication.

Printed in the United States of America
Library of Congress Cataloging-in-Publication data
Campbell, Darrel, 1957-

DARREL CAMPBELL
BIOGRAPHY

Darrel Campbell began his entertainment career attending the American Academy of Dramatic Arts in New York City and began his work as a professional TV and film actor in the city. Campbell launched his writing career in Los Angeles with NBC's *Days of Our Lives*. He developed literary, film and video products for Pistol Pete Maravich Enterprises, which included authoring the best-selling sports biography, *Heir to a Dream* (Gold Medallion Book Award winner) published by Thomas Nelson Publishers. After writing and producing the hit family film, *The Pistol: The Birth of a Legend,* Darrel was hired by television producer Matt Williams at Wind Dancer & Walt Disney Television to help develop new television products including NBC's *Carol and Company* starring Carol Burnett. Darrel served as an executive story editor for Wind Dancer and he wrote for ABC's comedy hit, *Home Improvement* starring Tim Allen. He was tapped by Walt Disney Animation to write the TV spin-off of *The Lion King,* penning the premiere episode of The *Lion King's Timon and Pumbaa* starring Nathan Lane. Darrel's animation writing includes *Tom and Jerry* for Renegade Animation, Cartoon Network and Warner Brothers Animation. Darrel also wrote and produced the family film, *Redemption of the Ghost*, starring John Savage, Rachel Hunter, Diane Ladd and Alexandra Paul. Darrel's show business experience includes songwriting, music producing, screenwriting, video and film producing, as well as acting and directing for film and television. Campbell, a drummer, is owner of Percussion Films, a vertically integrated company specializing in film, television, and publishing in order to create and develop high quality entertainment products.

Darrel Campbell

Follow Darrel Campbell at:

Facebook: Darrel Campbell @darrelcampbellauthor

Twitter: Darrel Campbell @dcampbellwriter

Email: Percussionfilmshq@gmail.com

Darrelcampbell.com

Darrel Campbell's books can be found on
Amazon.com

PERCUSSION

"Darrel Campbell, my longtime friend and colleague has an authenticity to his storytelling; a way of finding truth in an otherwise flawed world. Whether it was our years together on the #1 television series, Home Improvement, or our current days of creating content, he is a genuine person. He mentored me for many years in which I'm forever grateful. 'Hero & Friend: My Days with Pistol Pete Maravich' will inspire, motivate and appeal to all demographics because Pete was a leader of character and integrity—a man like we all should aspire to be."

Zachery Ty Bryan, Actor, Producer, Lost Lane Entertainment

"Darrel Campbell got the scoop of a lifetime when he was assigned to write Pete Maravich's autobiography, 'Heir to a Dream.' Campbell became much more than a writer to the basketball legend: a friend, a confidante and a conduit to one of the great American sports stories of the 20th Century. Three decades later comes Hero & Friend: My Days with Pistol Pete Maravich, the story behind the story and it's just as compelling."

Marshall Terrill, Co-author of Maravich

"For someone who grew up idolizing Pistol Pete Maravich, it's great to read new stories of his life. Author Darrel Campbell pens a captivating look at his time with Pete. Stories told in this new book give you an inside view of Pete's unique upbringing and exceptional life with his Coach/Dad, Press Maravich. A truly inspiring book about a man that was not only my hero but a hero to so many!"

Jackie Stiles, NCAA Scoring Champion & WNBA all-star basketball player

"I had an opportunity to meet Pete Maravich the day I tried out for the role of thirteen year old Pistol Pete, but sadly he past shortly thereafter. Luckily for me the work and love that Darrel Campbell put into the book 'Heir to a Dream' and 'Pistol Pete's Homework Basketball' provided me a window into Pete's life that I needed to take on the role of a lifetime." **Adam Guier, actor, young Pistol Pete, The Pistol: The Birth of a Legend**

DEDICATION

This book is dedicated to the memory of my good friend and childhood sports inspiration, Pistol Pete Maravich, and to his amazing father, Coach Peter "Press" Maravich. Both men taught me that knowledge isn't a monument to be kept for oneself, but a gift to be given to everyone seeking it. I also dedicate this work to the first heroes in my life, my parents. Jack and Josephine Campbell taught me that true heroic parents are those who devote their lives to being positively engaged in the lives of their children.

THANK YOU

I wish to thank Jackie Maravich, for always being a friend through the tough times and the good. Your love for your husband and young sons was an inspiration to me. Thanks for everything.

Thank you to my family: Pamela, Casey, Brock, Adelie, Brett, Sarah, Kellen and my mother, Josephine. Your love and laughter keep me balanced as my dreams constantly call me back to the cave.

A special thanks to Doug Pethoud and his family. My writing mentors, Matt Williams and Sheri Anderson. Friends and family who contributed to the effort and who encouraged me to the finish line: Zachery Ty Bryan, Rodney Stone, Marshall Terrill, Rodney Wood, Dr. Joe White, Coach Randy Stange, Jackie Stiles, Adam Guier, and my editors, Beth Berry and Doug Campbell and Adelie Cox.

TABLE OF CONTENTS

ACKNOWLEDGEMENTS

Thank you to all the "Pistol Pete" fans that helped make this book a possibility. My family has lived this legacy with me for over three decades. My wife, Pamela, and my children, Casey, Brock, Adelie and Brett grew up hearing "Pistol Pete" stories and emulating his skills so they could find even more enjoyment playing basketball or any other sport in which they participated.

Also, I must acknowledge the contributions to my life story that the Maravich family gave when our lives intersected at a wonderful, memorable and yet tragic time. Pete was a great son, husband, and father and his example encouraged me to be a better man. Pete told me that some day we would meet on the other side. Thanks, Pete. I look forward to that.

INTRODUCTION

For nearly thirty years I've approached my desk thinking to myself, "Someday, I should chronicle some of the most important days of my life—my days spent with Pistol Pete Maravich." The book would be about how a small-town American boy, the child of hard-working, middle-class parents, could grow up in the middle of nowhere, be inspired by a famous athlete, chase a dream, and then someday meet his inspirational childhood hero who had consumed so much of his youthful thoughts. More importantly, the book would reveal to the world a side of a beloved and iconic sports legend that few ever had the pleasure to know.

In my storage closet I recently discovered eight microcassette tapes consisting of conversations between Pete, his father and coach, Press Maravich, and myself, while I researched for the book, *Heir to a Dream* and the subsequent movie, *The Pistol: Birth of a Legend*. I also rummaged through my office file cabinets and found numerous folders of stories that Pete and Press told me or gave me during our friendship.

For years I have pondered what it might be like to share my story with sports enthusiasts. "Pistol Pete" memorabilia in my home theater provides me a daily reminder of Pete's life and what he and I experienced the last few years of his life. Thumbing through random notes from Pete and a carefully typed letter from his father, it struck me that if I found these things interesting there must be thousands more basketball and Pistol Pete Maravich fans that might find my story compelling too. Those research materials make up the bulk of this book.

When I met Pete Maravich I never imagined that I could become one of his closest confidantes and friends, nor did I imagine that I would witness the door of his life so suddenly slam shut. He was my childhood idol, my friend, my business partner, my mentor and my inspiration. In a second, his heart stopped beating, and I thought that all that I had acquired in the relationship was gone—all but the memories. As my life continued, I realized I had gained much more than the memories.

I discovered that Pete Maravich was a complex person. He had dodged death, suffered through tragedy, and attained wealth, fame, and love from adoring fans and family. There was also a spiritual and mystical component to the internal makeup of the unique American sports hero. I was privileged to experience much of the last few years of his life and what I saw, heard and experienced changed my life forever.

This book isn't a biography or autobiography. Pete and I wrote his memoir, *Heir to a Dream,* in 1986. This book is meant to be a look "behind-the-scenes" at a sports legend and unique human being away from the game he played. I attempt to share with the reader why I was so profoundly moved by his friendship and to share quotes from Pete that have never been either heard or written down by anyone else … until now.

PROLOGUE

"The most important thing in the world is family and love."
-John Wooden

When I was a boy, I had a hero—my dad. My father always told me stories of the bloody battles he fought in World War II (WWII). His older brother was his hero. My Uncle Freeman survived the D-Day invasion in France charging up Omaha Beach but was cut down six days later between the infamous hedgerows of Normandy. Uncle Freeman's unit had small white stars painted on the front of their helmets and when my father saw his brother for the last time laying in a body bag it was clear that an enemy bullet had found that star.

When my dad, Jack Campbell, entered France under the command of General George Patton, he fought valiantly with the image of his hero in his mind each day. My courageous dad found his way home after V-Day with medals of heroism and valor on his chest, but he walked through the rest of his life with an emotional hole in his heart because his brother had paid the ultimate price.

In 1984, my wife and I took my mom and dad to France to visit the Normandy American Military cemetery in Colleville-sur-Mer and that is where I first heard my dad say, *The boys in these graves are the real heroes.*

Much of my youth was spent wearing a pretend army uniform that my mother, Josephine, had purchased for me. She knew that I loved my hero and wanted to be as much like him as possible. My backyard was Normandy as I pretended to live the incredible stories my dad had shared with me.

1

On snowy winter days the backyard became Belgium during the Battle of the Bulge and it was the streets of Paris during V-day celebrations. My imagination took me to where my hero had been and where he experienced his amazing adventures.

My best memories are of my dad spending time with me. He was one of those guys who worked hard all day and no matter how fatigued he was, he would play catch or shoot baskets with me in the backyard. He taught me to hit a baseball, throw a curve and steal a base. For several years he was my little league baseball coach. I remember when he handed me my first baseball uniform. It was the 1960s and in those days the uniforms were heavy wool, just like the major league players wore. On the breast of my first gray wool jersey were the letters S.O.C.K.S.

Putting on my first baseball uniform had the same feeling to me as when I put on my green Army uniform. I felt important. I felt like I was somebody with a sense of identity and purpose. Having my dad personally hand me that uniform and then send me out to the pitcher's mound to win games for him solidified our bond of son and father.

I was born in Joplin, Missouri, and at age four my family moved to a tiny town a few miles east called Mount Vernon. Picture Mayberry on *The Andy Griffith Show* and you'll get a very accurate image. Most of the boys my age marked their months by what seasonal sport was in vogue. In the summer it was baseball. In September, we inflated the neglected football and we played in whoever's lawn had the least amount of trees. When winter turned to bitter cold and wet, we turned to the indoor sport we all loved—basketball.

One winter day, my dad brought home a tall light pole he had acquired from somewhere. Knowing him, he probably performed some electrical work for someone and got it instead of pay. The pole was aluminum just like the light poles lining Hickory Street in downtown Mount Vernon.

"What's that for?" I asked as Dad started digging a hole with his shovel.

"I'm putting up a basketball goal for you and your brothers."

"Wow, Dad! Thanks."

"I'll get you a backboard and a goal."

"And a net? Can we get a net?"

The basketball rims at the grade school playground never had nets, which made it hard to tell if the ball actually went through the circle of the iron rim.

"Yep. I'll get one. You practice hard and you can be like 'Pistol Pete,'" Dad nodded.

I wasn't sure who "Pistol Pete" was, but if Dad said I could be like someone, then I figured "Pistol Pete" must be someone to look up to.

My father was a quiet man of few words. When he was a child during the Great Depression, I think his father was harsh and gruff. It was obvious to me that this gentle hero had set out to treat my brothers and me in a kinder and gentler manner than he had been treated.

My Dad would tell me, "When my dad came home, sometimes I would hide under the front porch. He was unhappy a lot. Dad died when I was in the Army."

"What about Grandma?" I asked. I had never known his mother or his father. My grandparents were gone long before I was born.

"Your grandma worked herself to death."

"What do you mean?"

"It was the Great Depression. She had ten kids and not enough food. All I remember is how much she worked. She taught me to cook, so when she died, I quit high school after the ninth grade so I could help cook and feed everyone. My brothers and sisters went out and did whatever they could to make a few cents a day."

I pondered my hero's childhood reality often when I watched him doing manual labor. He was amazing. He wore the name, "Jack," well because he was truly a Jack-of-all-trades. I'm sure as a child of the Great Depression he had to be resourceful if he wanted something. He could repair cars, pour concrete, wire a house, plumb a house, put on a roof, paint walls and install cabinets. When he built a two-story addition onto our house, he added two bedrooms, a bath, and a family room downstairs where we could gather. We had never had a fireplace and Dad wanted one for my mother to enjoy at Christmas time. I loved to watch my dad work and that's how I learned to work on the houses I've owned as an adult.

Even the way my dad dug a hole in the ground was somewhat spectacular to my young mind. With a long-handled shovel, he would place his foot just right on the rim of the shovel, push it down with tremendous force and easily spade out of the ground a large chunk of dirt.

"How do you do that so easy, Dad?"

"Do what?"

"Shovel dirt like that?"

Questions to my hero often would illicit more than a brief answer. He would launch into stories about digging. During the Great Depression, digging ditches was how he and Freeman made fifty cents a day to keep food on the table.

In the Army Dad lived with a shovel connected to his backpack and the foxholes he dug with it saved his life. He kept a U.S. Army shovel in the garage and I always thought it was like a mini-shovel intended for digging little holes.

With the hole dug to his satisfaction, Dad lifted the tall aluminum pole and slid it into the prepared resting place, landing with a chunk.

"You know, up in Northern Missouri, they have to buy rocks, their dirt is so black," Dad said, with a sigh.

Dad pulled out the pole and grabbed a four-foot long steel bar. He slammed that bar into the hole over and over to break up the stubborn rocks. He let me fish out a few of the pieces but then he took over and cleaned the hole again. His hands were rough and strong. I remember after a long day of hard labor he would wash his hands and then pull a bottle of "Cornhusker's Lotion" from the medicine cabinet.

"My hands are as rough as corn cobs," Dad said, as he bathed his hands with the lotion.

I put out my hands and Dad dripped a couple of dollops of "Cornhuskers" on my hands. If my hero put that stuff on his hands, I would do the same. To this day, I can still smell the aroma of that lotion.

Dad got the pole inserted into the hole and then mixed concrete in his rusty wheelbarrow. I sprayed in a small amount of water as he moved the rocky cement mix back and forth with a hoe. Crunch, crunch, crunch the sand and mix moved. When the concrete was ready, he tipped the wheelbarrow and the hole was filled with just the right amount of mix that would keep my first basketball goal firmly in place.

The next day, I walked out into the backyard to discover that Dad had already fashioned the backboard and goal to the post.

5

As he finished bolting the orange rim into the wood, I remember how incredibly high he was as he stood on his rickety wooden ladder. He was putting a net on the rim for me.

"Thanks for the net, Dad.

"The rim looks a lot bigger from up here."

"How high is it, Dad?"

"The rim is ten feet, just like a real basketball court."

Dad unhooked his tape measure from his belt and did a quick measurement. He placed the ruler against the rim.

"Hold the bottom to the ground there," Dad instructed. After a moment, Dad grunted. "Hmm. How did that happen?"

"What is it?"

"About ten-foot-two-inches."

Dad didn't have to tell me that. He could have kept his mistake to himself, but he was a simple, honest and transparent man. To me, he never made mistakes, but to him, a mistake was something that he had to own up to and admit.

I surveyed the dirt and grass that would have to serve as my basketball court.

"It's perfect!" I shouted.

Of course it was all far from perfect. I had to learn to dribble the ball over clumps of grass and sometimes in mud after a rain. I suppose when I told him it was "perfect" I really meant that my life was feeling perfect. My dad, my hero, loved me and had built me a place to shoot baskets.

I played a lot of basketball, but being the shortest kid in my class didn't bode well for becoming a powerhouse basketball player. I've often joked that had I been taller, faster, quicker, more proficient and more talented I could have made it to the pros! When I was young and playing on my junior high team, I believed that I could accomplish whatever I set my mind to.

I always loved basketball even though our only exposure to the game was our local high school team. To their credit, our Mount Vernon Mountaineer team was one of the best in the state and the rows of large green and white championship banners hanging in the gym were constant reminders.

My coach, Coach L.M. Carson, was a high school all-American. His son, Ron, was an All-American who turned down an offer to play professionally because there wasn't that much money to be made in the sport at that time. Coach Carson's younger son, Tim, was the closest thing to Pete Maravich that any of us had ever witnessed. He could shoot, pass and dribble a lot like Pete and during his years in high school it was hard to find a seat in the stadium because Tim put on a show.

Also, to put things into historical perspective, in the 1960s finding a basketball game on television while living in the Ozarks was a near impossibility. There were only three networks to be found on our old Magnavox black and white TV, and those three networks; CBS, ABC, and NBC, only came in clear if our outdoor antenna was facing the right direction. Sometimes we could catch a glimpse of the floppy-socked kid named Pete Maravich, when our local sports reporters talked about the nation's leading scorer playing at Louisiana State University.

My best friend, Roger, found articles in the *Springfield News Leader* or the *Joplin Globe,* and before long he was growing his hair so he would look more like Pete Maravich. The day Roger walked out of the locker room with baggy socks bunched down around both ankles I realized Pete was influencing many of us who played basketball. There was something cool and different about the "Elvis" of basketball as some sports reporters were calling him.

Pete was changing the way we thought about the sport. He was an innovator making the sport more exciting to watch and more fun to play. For the next several years, Pistol Pete Maravich was my sports hero. He was the player that many of my friends and I wanted to emulate. No one before him dribbled the way Pete did. He could shoot from almost anywhere with defenders all over him, and his passes were otherworldly. When I was a teenager he was the player I looked up to and who I wanted to imitate. I often wished I could go to a game and watch the wizard of basketball in person.

As I followed his career through college and then the NBA, I always imagined what it would be like to meet my sports hero. I wondered what we would talk about. I also wondered what it would be like to be his friend—not just an acquaintance or a fan, but his close friend. Little did I know that my youthful imaginations would someday become reality. This is the story of how it happened.

CHAPTER 1
A Childhood Inspiration

In the late 1960s *Sports Illustrated* was the number one sports magazine publication in America, and in our house the glossy color periodical was nearly sacred. My brother had to sell magazines as a fundraiser for our high school band. Sometimes Doug let me tag along with him as he walked door-to-door and ask people to buy subscriptions to magazines such as *Better Homes and Gardens*, *Newsweek*, *Boy's Life* and *Sports Illustrated*. With the money raised, the school band could buy new instruments for the program.

My brother always made sure he talked Mom and Dad into buying a subscription to *Sports Illustrated*. We rarely had money for anything extra, so if Mom turned down my brother's request, Doug would use his money from mowing lawns to make sure that the precious sports magazine showed up in our mailbox. Besides my best friend Roger's idolization of "Pistol Pete," my brother's simple purchase of *S.I.* was the primary way I learned about a college basketball phenomenon named Pete Maravich; a player who was playing hoops for his dad and breaking college records as a sophomore at LSU.

Forty-four points a game? That was the craziest thing we had ever heard. We were aware of professional players scoring that much; Wilt Chamberlain, Bill Russell and those guys, but this was a college kid averaging forty-four a night! When I viewed a montage of "Pistol Pete" pictures on the cover of the March 4, 1968 edition of *Sports Illustrated* it was forever emblazoned in my mind. The large middle picture is Pete standing with his father, Coach Press Maravich.

In the picture Press is in the act of spouting his game instructions to his son, the star player. Around the center picture are four more pictures: Pete throwing a no-look pass, Pete dribbling and Pete screeching to a stop before shooting. In the right-hand corner, completing the montage is Pete sailing through the air about to hook in or lay in the basketball.

"Okay, that's the guy dad was talking about. That's who I want to be," I told my brother. My remark was probably repeated verbatim by millions of little brothers from coast to coast in the United States.

Doug looked at me as if I were an alien and said, "You're going to have to learn to beat me first."

Doug challenged me to a game of H-O-R-S-E and we ran outside to our new basketball goal. As usual, I lost. Doug challenged me to a game of one-on-one. Again, I lost. My brother was much bigger than my boney, short frame and when he had the ball on offense, he would stick his buttocks into me and dribble backwards toward the goal forcing me in the direction his rear end would push! He was the bulldozer and I was like the snow being removed from the street. He forced his way under the goal and casually flipped in the shot as I struggled to jump and block the ball. Yes, that's how I was smeared by him every game as a child.

Our games of one-on-one became more competitive as I got older and I could make my jump shots. I also learned how to shoot those twelve-foot hook shots like "Pistol Pete" did on occasion. That's how I started challenging my brother and how I began enjoying basketball. By the time I made it to the junior varsity and varsity teams my shot was what would be considered a three-pointer today. The main reason for that approach was because I was still the shortest guy in my class and I didn't want taller players to reject my shot.

10

In junior high, shooting from "a mile away" became my trademark. By then, I had witnessed "Pistol Pete" shooting from long distance and I wanted to be just like him.

For reasons that will remain private, when I was playing sports in high school I was given the nicknames "Bod" and "Bodney." My oldest friends from high school days still call me "Bod." When Coach Pendleton or Coach Breeden or Coach Carson would graciously put me in the game, the cheerleaders would chant, "Bodney, Bodney, Bodney." It was both motivating and a bit embarrassing, but I realized they wanted me to launch my trademark jump shot from 30 feet or some other ridiculous distance. The way I figured it, if I was the guard bringing the ball across half court I was in my range.

Shots from long range were one of "Pistol Pete's" trademarks. When we saw Pete more often on Saturday broadcasts of NBA games in the early 1970s, there were times that the camera missed Pete's shot because he was truly out of frame. Pete was becoming someone idolized as a sports hero. As a result, Roger and I grew our hair even longer and we had our hair cut like Pete's Beatle-styled hair. Floppy socks and long hair by that time had become solidly Pete's visual trademark. Shooting from anywhere, making unimaginable passes and dribbling like no other player before were "Pistol Pete's" playing trademark … well, at least Roger and I had the socks and hair.

Oscar Wilde famously wrote, "Imitation is the sincerest form of flattery that mediocrity can pay to greatness."

Never was a thought so spot-on in the case of those who wished to emulate the great Pistol Pete Maravich. We wanted to look like him and play like him. At that time in my wonder years, I could only dream to meet him and become his friend. I never truly believed that day would arrive.

CHAPTER 2

A Chance to Meet

When Roger died suddenly, the air was taken out of many of my dreams. It was the summer before our freshman year in college. He and I talked about playing professional baseball or traveling to far-off lands to work as archeologists, but when we graduated high school we agreed that we were best suited for the radio and television business to become successful doing what we loved to do.

At that time in my life there was no one closer to me. With his death ever present in my thoughts I entered college with a broken spirit and a painted-on smile. I chose to put all my lofty and far-fetched dreams of playing sports on a shelf. Playing basketball was never really an option, although I continued watching every game I could. Baseball might have been an option in college, but my musical and theatrical interests, especially comedy-writing and performing, had taken precedence in my life and performing arts were beginning to consume my time.

Four years of college seemed to fly by. After I earned a degree in theater and English I left my little town in Missouri and moved to New York City to pursue my dreams of being in show business. I began my formal training at the American Academy of Dramatic Arts in Manhattan. If I wasn't going to be in the U.S. Army like my dad or be a basketball player like "Pistol Pete," or be a drummer for the Beatles (Ringo would never retire), it was my desire to become a professional actor on Broadway and then transition to movies in Hollywood. That was my plan.

After seven years of working professionally as an actor on the East Coast, my college sweetheart and new bride, Pamela, and I agreed that I should chase my dream in Los Angeles.

Note to reader: "Make sure you marry a person who supports your dream."

After four years of playing the role of Peter Davidson on the soap opera Another Life, I wanted to head west and break into the Hollywood acting scene. We moved into a small apartment in Studio City, California, and Pam and I started a new adventure.

Pam got a job as a writer's assistant for Sheri Anderson, the head writer on the soap opera *Days of Our Lives*. After a few weeks Pam advanced to working daily with a staff of creative soap opera writers.

Meanwhile, my days were full of acting auditions and working out in the gym. One afternoon after a discouraging audition at Universal Studios, I came home and pondered the status of my life. I had been acting professionally for seven years and was actually making a good living at it, but in many ways I felt as if I was starting over after moving to Los Angeles.

Pam came home from Sunset Gower Studios one day and as usual she was cheery and full of stories.

"Hey, guess who I met in the hallway at work?" Pam asked.

"Who?"

Pam handed me a small blue piece of paper. On it I read the signature of a man that I had for years watched play football on TV. "O.J. Simpson," the signature read.

"O.J.? No kidding."

"He was working on the studio lot and when I saw him, I just thought I'd ask him to sign something."

"What was he like?"

"He was really nice and he gave me that," Pam explained.

A few years later O.J.'s greatest scramble would be in a white Bronco on an L.A. freeway and not running down a football field. Pam's encounter with O.J. was another irritation for me. She was enjoying a successful career at NBC while I was sitting at home waiting for the phone to ring. Then it dawned on me to ask:

"How much do the writers make on that show?"

"Hundreds of thousands," Pam replied.

"I mean, how about the dialogue writers? Like, the bottom rung writers. I have an English degree. I've written comedy scripts," I remarked.

When I was an actor on *Another Life*, the first cable soap opera in the U.S., I was aware that the writers of that show were very good. However, they must have squirmed when they heard their lines changed by me each week. Sitting in the green room with me during those early soap opera days was a brilliant screenwriter named Matt Williams who would go on to produce *The Cosby Show* and then create *Roseanne* and *Home Improvement*.

Matt was a New York-based actor and burgeoning playwright. He played my brother-in-law in the soap opera, and each week, he and I would tweak the scripts in which we were acting. We spent hours in the green room discussing things like story structure and character development until we had to go on the set and act out our scenes.

14

I know those formative hours didn't make me a great writer, but the valuable time with Matt gave me confidence and later it led to my working with him at Walt Disney Television as a screenwriter. Matt became one of my closest friends and still is to this day.

"How much do they get paid?" I asked Pam.

"One-thousand-seven-hundred and fifty dollars an episode," Pam replied.

"One-thousand-seven-hundred-fifty?" I exclaimed. "That's about one-thousand-seven-hundred and fifty dollars more than I'm making now! Maybe I could do two a week."

"Don't get too excited, or greedy. Let me see what I can do," Pam replied.

After a discussion with her bosses, Sheri Anderson and Leah Leiman, Pam informed me that I would have to write a "spec" script first. That simply meant that I would take a crack at writing a full script without being paid. And she added that writers who are members of the Writers Guild of America are usually considered before non-members. I was not a member, but like my father picking up that piece of steel and cracking rocks, I had learned that obstacles are to be shattered.

"Can you get me an outline? And a script I can read to see the formatting? I'll write a spec script."

"Sure. I'll talk to Sheri and Leah tomorrow and tell them you'd like to do that."

Leah Leiman and Sheri Anderson were head writers for *Days of Our Lives*, and to this day we consider Leah and Sheri to be some of our dearest friends. They sent Pam home with an outline and instructions that they would give me a few days to write the speculative script. "Spec" scripts are like a written tryout or audition to discover if the writer has what it takes to write the show.

I had a beautiful inside track to the job. Pam had been Sheri Anderson's writing assistant before taking on the duties of script production coordinator for the writers.

Pam and I had become personal friends of Sheri and we spent time going to dinners and sailing on weekends.

When I first visited with Sheri about writing for her on Days of Our Lives, I was sitting on the balcony of her condo in Malibu watching the waves roll on and off the beach.

"Any words of wisdom, Sheri?"

"I'll tell you what I was told when I got started as a soap writer," Sheri replied without hesitation. "Go for the emotion."

That seemed like a simple note, but as I have continued my film and TV career, I realize just how perfect that piece of advice was for me because I have used that suggestion often. I have witnessed audiences in theaters give my movies standing ovations. It's not that I'm a great writer, but I understand that people wish to be moved by stories. Thank you, Sheri.

At the time, Pam and I lived in a studio apartment on Aqua Vista Street in Studio City. The head writer loaned me an electric typewriter, and since Pam and I didn't have much furniture in our first L.A. apartment, I set the IBM Selectric on the arm of the couch, pulled up a chair and began typing. As I wrote, I could distinctly hear in my mind each of the characters saying my lines. I had watched the show so long that writing dialogue came easily to me. One hundred pages later, and a lot of White Out to cover my errors, I had my first spec script completed. Because I didn't know any better, I remember lacing funny moments into the dramatic soap opera script because I felt it would be more like real life.

I really enjoyed the show and I couldn't help but recall how when I was a child my mother would peel potatoes into a big red bowl as she and I watched *Days of Our Lives* on our old black and white TV screen. I was very familiar with the characters, played famously by people like MacDonald Carey and Frances Reid.

"*Days*," as all the real fans call it, was my Mom's "story." She watched it religiously for years and still does as I write this book.

My approach to writing the script was to write it as if the characters were real, three-dimensional people, regardless of their age, type or even stereotype. In other words, I would have Doctor Horton (Mac Carey), talk to his wife, Alice (Francis Reid), as if he was truly in love with her and still sexually attracted to her after their forty-plus years of marriage. The result was fresh performances for the veterans of the show. I also wrote some whimsical moments in my "spec" episode that were a bit different for the actors to play. It was a dream for me to be involved in show business at any level, and having a shot at being a writer for one of the longest-running shows in television history helped me throw caution to the wind.

Pam came home with a smile on her face and announced, "They loved your script!"

"What? Don't kid me. I need really good news."

"Really. They loved it. They laughed and they loved the relationships and witty dialogue."

"And?"

"And they're offering you a contract to write the show," Pam added with a hug.

"We can eat better food and pay for this apartment!" I joked.

17

That speculative script led to my writing over sixty episodes of my mother and father's favorite soap opera. I remember when my parents came out to Hollywood and had the wonderful pleasure meeting the stars they had watched for decades on TV. Coming home for lunch to watch *Days* with my mother was one of my dad's daily rituals.

I'll never forget the look on Mom and Dad's faces when they met the lovely and gracious Diedre Hall who plays Marlena on the show. She visited with my parents as if they were her long-lost family. When hugs and kisses followed their visit I realized then why Deidre had the most fans in daytime television.

The months passed and one afternoon my phone rang. At the time I was sitting at my desk writing a *Days of Our Lives* script. Pam was pregnant with our first baby and life for us was going well.

"Darrel Campbell's office," I answered.

"Hey, it's Frank," the voice on the other end of the line announced.

Frank Schroeder, the husband of our production secretary on my old soap opera, *Another Life*, was a golfing buddy that I challenged often on the golf courses on the East coast.

"Hey, D, what would you say to writing a movie about Pistol Pete Maravich?" he asked.

"Really? The Pistol?"

"I just produced a TV show and he was the guest. I think we can get him to agree to a movie."

"I'm in," I told Frank without hesitation.

I was coming to the end of my *Days* contract and the timing couldn't have been better. I mean, yes, I could have kept writing soaps, but my goal had always been to be involved in movies, and I figured that this could be my chance.

18

Frank told me that he had struck up a friendship with Maravich, who had been a bit of a recluse for several years. Actually, he had been out of the public eye since walking away from professional basketball at age thirty. Frank was producing a TV show on ESPN starring Doctor J. as host, and "Pistol Pete" was his guest.

It was a rare interview because Pete had been living privately at his home in Covington, Louisiana. His days of driving fast cars and making millions were over and he was married and raising a family. Pete had been out of the limelight for a while and he preferred it that way.

"I want you to meet Pete and talk it over," Frank requested.

The phone call ended. I had committed myself to leaving daytime television writing and stepping into the unpredictable and risky world of independent filmmaking. Why? I had a chance to meet my childhood hero and perhaps make a movie about him.

I gently informed Pam of my decision and she smiled a forced smile I had seen before. It was her devoted wife smile that communicated, "I'm not sure what you're thinking, but I support you."

It wasn't a glowing endorsement, but it would do.

CHAPTER 3
Sudden Connection

Fountain Valley, California - 1985

An introductory meeting was set for the legendary American sports icon and me. I was to drive to Fountain Valley, California, where I would find Pete Maravich. He was working out in a basketball gymnasium and would be expecting me. Pete had agreed to come out of retirement for a short period of time to play a few exhibition basketball games with the great Harlem Globetrotter, Meadowlark Lemon, and a team he called "The Shooting Stars." I was reminded that back in the early days of Pete's professional career that The Harlem Globetrotters had asked Maravich to become the first white player to join them. I could only imagine "Pistol Pete" playing with that extraordinary group of shooters and ball-handlers. His flashy basketball style would have certainly fit.

It was a warm fall afternoon when I walked into the gym in Fountain Valley to meet my sports hero. I wondered what he would be like. Would he be out-going and gregarious or would he be like some of the TV stars I work with who are charismatic on camera but keep to themselves and barely speak in person?

There were no chairs in the room, but there was a six-foot-long table with folding legs at the edge of the court. Some of the Shooting Stars players kept their gym bags and other items on the table. I scanned the room and among the dozen or so African-American basketball players the lone tall Caucasian player was easy to spot.

There he was—the legendary "Pistol Pete"—dribbling back and forth between his legs casually performing what I would later learn was his famous scissor drill. In a heartbeat, he pulled up and shot his jump shot he had made famous. My first thought was, "Why in the world did he retire at age thirty? This guy can still shoot like the forty-four point-a-game player I watched on TV.

After a few minutes, Pete saw me standing courtside. He nodded to me and I expected him to say something like, "Hey, you must be Darrel Campbell, my screenwriter!" That's the way I would have written the moment had I been writing the scene, but real life has a way of humbling Hollywood creatives.

The moment was actually more like this: Pete sauntered over as I leaned against the folding table. I think my hand had been shaking for a while.

By this time in my life, having lived in New York City around the Broadway theatrical community and a few years in Los Angeles working for NBC, I had met a few stars—the cast of *Days of Our Lives* for starters. On other occasions I had met famous actors and actresses such as Geraldine Page, Mary Martin, Jennifer Aniston, Jason Robards and Kirk Douglas. I had shaken the hand of President George W. Bush.

But, this moment was different. It was very personal. I was meeting my hero Pistol Pete Maravich. I was about to go into business with the superstar I had pretended to be when I was a child. And he was standing in front of me.

"Hi," Pete greeted me with a nod.

"Hi, Pete."

"How's it going?"

"Great."

"You go to school here?" Pete asked me.

Go to school here? I thought, *did he just ask if I was a student at this school? Yes. Yes, he did.*

"I'm Darrel Campbell. I'm writing a movie about your life," I smiled as I shook his hand.

Pete laughed, and I think he was also embarrassed by the faux pas.

"You look pretty young."

"Looking young has served me well," I replied.

I later told him that for my first recurring acting job on TV I played a sixteen-year-old. I was twenty-three when I signed that contract.

"You look like you're still in high school."

"You look like you should still be playing pro ball."

"Looks are deceiving."

Pete grabbed his gear and we drove to a nearby restaurant to have lunch and get to know each other. I ordered a burger and Pete ordered grilled salmon. It wasn't long before he was advising me about how I should begin a more nutritious diet. Pete was thin. His eyes were sunken with dark rings around them, which made me question his advice.

"So you're writing my movie?"

"Yes, sir."

"You think my life would make a good movie?"

"I do."

"I was in a movie, ya know. Not a good one, but I was in it," Pete laughed, referring to a lowbrow comedy he filmed in the late 1970s called *Scoring*. "I don't want to tell my whole story." Pete continued, "There are things I will leave out because I don't want to hurt anyone. Some things are way too private."

"I understand."

"Plus, my real life is pretty boring."

I couldn't believe he uttered those words. I would learn later just how humble "Pistol Pete" had become after his retirement from the game.

I could also tell this hero of mine was no shallow man. His furrowed brow and his concentration were intense and intimidating. I sat quietly and let him offer his thoughts without interruption. What Pete said next set the tone for the rest of our conversations. Pete's thoughts ran deep, and he wasn't afraid to tell me what was on his mind.

"My mother killed herself," Pete continued with no warning or transition.

"Oh, I'm sorry. I didn't know."

"It's part of my story I want to tell, and as hard as that may be for me, I want people to know."

"Sure."

"My mother was so beautiful. I'll find a picture for you."

"Okay."

"I have nightmares about her. I don't know if she is in heaven or being tormented in hell."

I kept chewing my food, unsure of how I was to keep up my side of this conversation. I reminded myself that this was a time for him to download information and history to me. Pete was the subject of the movie or book and I was the scribe. "Book?" It was at that moment that I remember thinking; *this might not be just a movie project. Should this be a book? But, I'm not an author!* I began to sweat. I tried to figure out how to push the conversation back to filmmaking—an arena in which I could compete. A discussion about making a film was where I could control the tempo of the game, not let him dribble around me with wild subject matter that was off the subject.

23

"Is my mother falling into a bottomless pit of blackness? Is she screaming for help? I can't get to her. I can't help her. You know why hell is so black, Darrel? It is absent of God. God is light and in Him there is no darkness. I cry sometimes for my mother. I think about her place in eternity."

I soon realized that Pete was the kind of guy who asks questions but doesn't really expect the other person to answer. He was simply letting his thoughts flow and like playing basketball, he could go left or right with the same intensity and confidence.

"God is sovereign, right, Darrel? I mean, maybe she knew Jesus enough to escape hell? She was an alcoholic, and so I always say that wasn't my mother who killed herself. Know what I mean? That wasn't her who pulled that trigger. It was someone else. My mother was so sweet. She was so caring and she loved her family and me so much. She wouldn't have done that ... not to herself or to me. She just wouldn't."

"What was your mom's name?"

"Helen. Helen Maravich. One of my sense memories is the smell of her perfume. She always smelled so good," Pete continued quietly as he stared out the window. "You want dessert?"

"Do you?"

"Sugar is a killer."

"Oh, right. I read that somewhere. I guess not. I'm good."

"Check please?" Pete motioned to the waiter.

The waiter walked over with the check.

"Sorry. I was talking to the guys in the kitchen. Are you who I think you are?" the young man asked.

"Yes. Probably," Pete replied.

24

"'Pistol Pete? Could I have your autograph?" the waiter asked as he put a piece of paper and a pen on the table.

Pete signed his name on the paper and the waiter graciously accepted it and walked away with our bill and Pete's credit card. With his wallet still on the table, Pete retrieved his Louisiana driver's license and held it up for me to see.

"Have you ever thought that as Christians, we are citizens of heaven? I mean; it's like we have an ID like this ... like a drivers license that has our picture and name on it, but where mine says 'Covington, Louisiana,' my new one will say 'H.e.a.v.e.n.,' Heaven."

"I've never really thought about it."

"We should feel good about that. It should be something that keeps us happy all day," Pete finished his thought. He took a drink of water and looked me in the eyes. Again he asked, "So, do you think my life will make a good movie?"

"I do. I mean, I don't know the whole story, but I think it will."

"I don't want it to be all about me."

"What do you mean? It's your story."

"It's more about my dad, really. You know, when your father is your coach and your coach is your father, it's hard. The lines get blurred."

"My dad was my little league coach."

Pete laughed. I immediately wanted to grab those words I had just uttered and put them back in my mouth.

"Yeah, that was a dumb thing to say; I mean, there's no comparison ..."

"No. That's okay," Pete assured me. "You should be proud of your dad and you obviously are."

"Yes. He was a bit of a World War Two hero. I mean, I think so, anyway."

"My dad was a pilot—World War Two. Speaking of pilots, I have to catch a plane back home. You should come to Louisiana and meet my family.

"I'd like that."

"You really think we have a movie here?"

"We'll see."

"Darrel, if we're going to do this, I really want to make a movie of hope."

"Hope?"

"Yes. I want the audience to watch the screen and be mesmerized by things that happened to me – things I did as a kid. They should be inspired to pursue their dreams like I did mine. I want them to walk out the back of the theater with hope in their hearts. If they don't leave with hope, then we've really messed up the movie."

I had never heard it put that way; "a movie of hope." It was Pete's down-home, Southern way of telling me that his story was not sad, but a story of desire and determination to overcome the trials in his life. It was his desire for people to feel good because they had watched the movie. He didn't want to sugar coat his life, but tell a truthful tale that would resonate with persons of all ages.

Pete shook my hand and we said goodbye. My first meeting with him concluded and my head was swimming with excitement and thoughts of the new direction my life was taking. I shut the door to my car and I sat there in silence.

What did I get myself into? I wondered. *How could I possibly do justice to the story of my childhood sports hero?* I looked into the rearview mirror and slipped on my Wayfarer sunglasses. I thought I looked like Tom Cruise in the film *Risky Business* as I stared in the mirror trying to soak it all in.

26

Finally, I let out a shout and laughed, *Holy cow! I'm writing my first feature film. I'm writing my first feature film and it's about Pistol Pete Maravich. Are you kidding me? Wait! I just had lunch with Pistol Pete Maravich! Shoulda brought a camera.*

Cranking up my stereo I let the two subs mounted in the back seat reverberate my entire body as I celebrated with some Bryan Adams music blasting my ears. I jumped on the 118 Freeway and headed back to Studio City. I shuddered with excitement.

I was living a dream.

CHAPTER 4

To Louisiana

"What was he like?" Pam asked.

"Pete was a lot like what I expected and yet, in some ways he was a total surprise. I really like him as a person, and I think he likes me. It's weird, but I felt as if we had been friends for a long time. He wants to get together again and get this project rolling."

"Seriously?"

"Yes. He's pretty amazing."

"In what way?"

"Well, out of all the things that Pete and I talked about during our first meeting, I can't get over what he said about his mother. I had been warned that "Pistol Pete" was not one for small talk. He didn't mind diving into difficult metaphysical subject matter. He's afraid his mother is in hell."

"Oh, my. He said that?" Pam asked.

"Yes. I've never met anyone like this guy."

"That's so sad."

"Yes. He's really tormented by it. He blew me away, Pam. Pete's brilliant. I don't know what I expected. I heard he was into a lot of things like UFO's and the Bible and other things, but he's so much more. This is going to be a great project. I feel it."

A few days later I was on a plane to Louisiana. It was nerve-racking preparing for our next interview, but it was pure excitement, too. Frank picked me up at the airport and he was as thrilled as I was when he parked his black Ford Granada outside the Maravich home.

I put a fresh tape in my mini-cassette recorder and we headed for the front porch.

The house was a large two-story Victorian that Pete had remodeled from the ground up. It was, and still is, a magnificent house that fits perfectly in the American Deep South. Frank knocked on the door and after a few moments the large front door opened to reveal Pete's 6'5" frame.

"Hey, you made it!" Pete remarked as he looked down at me.

Six-foot-five had never looked as tall to me as when Pete stood there in the doorway. I'm not sure why he seemed so much taller than the first time we met in California. This was Pete's domain that he had remodeled for himself. He had doorways and doors transformed into super-size. The ceilings were high in the whole house. It had an *Alice in Wonderland* feel to me as I looked around at the perfect architecture.

As I entered the foyer, I saw Pete's home office. There were books on shelves and a large desk in the room. Pete invited me in as if I were being interviewed for a job.

"Sweet office," I told him as I looked around the beautifully appointed room.

I had expected pictures of Pete to be covering the walls. But, there were no images of Pete and U.S. presidents and no snapshots of Pete and his famous athlete friends; not even an eight-by-ten of Pete dribbling the ball on the court.

There were books, but not about sports. On his desk sat an open Bible. The pages were dog-eared and it was obvious that the book was one in which he had spent a great deal of time delving into.

"Go on, son. Go play," Pete instructed as he looked under his desk.

Suddenly, Pete's four-year-old son, Joshua scrambled out on his hands and knees and out of the room. Pete smiled.

"My goal is to teach my kids a thousand Bible verses before they leave high school."

I wasn't surprised by his comment. Pete was a goal setter and never did anything in an insignificant way. He lived his life to extremes. He played hard and lived hard. Just as he had pushed his physical skills to the highest level of his sport, he had also pushed his thoughts and imagination to the limit. He had never been a scholar athlete, but he had dedicated himself to be a scholar in life. As an adult he was a sponge for learning and his wisdom was evident.

"I really want my boys to learn ten thousand Bible verses, but they have to start somewhere."

"You like reading?" I asked.

"I do. Mainly the Word. I didn't used to like reading. I hated school work, but I got interested in lots of things once I got into the pros. Oh, man, I jumped in deep into ufology; read everything I could find."

"Ufology? Like, aliens?" I wondered.

"Oh, yeah. I would go outside at night and invite aliens to land on my roof. I actually thought that would happen someday."

The expression on my face must have communicated my skepticism.

"You think I'm joking? They might be out there somewhere in the vastness of space. We would be the most arrogant beings in the universe to believe that God couldn't create some other life forms. Someday, we'll all see. When I look up to the stars, I remember the Bible says that God 'flung the stars into space…' Like I would toss a basketball. God's power and majesty is unfathomable."

I hated to break his train of thought, but I had something important to do.

"It's been a long trip. Can I use your restroom?"

"Out that door and to the left," Pete gestured.

I didn't want to miss any more of his unexpected pronouncements, but I had to excuse myself. The first thing I noticed when I entered the hallway restroom was this it was not your regular toilet with a normal-sized john.

In fact, it was my first visit to what I would call a water closet. High over the porcelain seat was a large wooden box. Hanging from the box was a brass chain with a wooden handle.

After I took care of business, I looked up at the handle and thought; *I sure hope that's how you flush this toilet.* I gave the handle a tug and water loudly gushed into the john. I stood and watched it like a hick from the sticks who had never seen a flushing toilet. I washed my hands, dried them and opened the bathroom door. Standing in the hallway was "Pistol Pete" leaning against the doorframe.

"Could you reach the chain? I was worried about you."

Before I could reply, Pete burst into laughter that would become familiar to me. It was an infectious laugh that seemed to invite everyone else in the room to join him.

Okay, he's a joker; a teaser; he likes to laugh, I thought. For a guy like me who enjoys writing comedy and watching comedy films and television, that's an important trait in a person with whom I'll be spending lots of time.

Pete invited us to take an impromptu tour of his home. Nothing was left to chance. Beautiful wood floors were everywhere. A tall staircase greeted guests as they walked into the foyer. The wooden steps led to an indoor gym.

We walked up the stairs and when we entered the gym I noticed small basketball goals had been mounted on the walls for each of his boys.

"I'm teaching my sons *Homework Basketball*."

"What's that?" I asked.

"It's a name my dad and I came up with to help young players get better at fundamentals. Pop taught me hundreds of dribbling, passing and shooting drills when I was little and they're the same drills I used all through my college and pro years."

Pete's seven-year-old boy, Jaeson, sported Pete-like long hair and dribbled into the room.

"Show Darrel your figure eight drill," Pete encouraged.

His oldest boy was shy, but with perfect attention and obedience to his father the youngster stood with his legs spread apart and began to dribble proficiently. He dribbled around one leg, then through his legs and around the other leg in a figure eight. Round and round he dribbled without a hitch.

"He's practicing several hours a day."

"It shows."

"My dad turned me into a basketball android when I was my son's age. I'm trying not to do that to my boys, but I know that the more they practice the better they will be. It's like if I read a book ten thousand times and you read it a couple of times, which one of us will know the book better? You get what I'm saying?"

"Sure. Whoever practices the most should be the best."

"Yes. But it's not just the most. It's whoever practices the most in the right way. A guy can hit a thousand golf balls at the driving range every day, but if he is hitting a thousand balls incorrectly, what good is that?"

32

Pete's Homework Basketball is made up of teaching the right fundamentals and techniques. Practicing fundamentals right, thousands of times a day, makes the player exceptional.

"Exceptional" was just one of the words that came to mind as I watched and listened to one story after another. It was an author's dream to have a subject who, quite frankly, wouldn't stop talking about who he was and what he believed. He wasn't bragging at all; he was enthusiastic about sharing what he knew and what he had experienced. I detected a strange urgency to his story telling. It was as if the game clock was ticking and the tempo of translating his stories from his memory to me was limited. Pete picked up a ball and dribbled it between his legs and then spun it on his finger. With the ball spinning, he took the ball behind his back and through his legs where he changed hands and continued spinning the ball on his other index finger.

"Can you do that, Darrel?"

"I cannot."

We laughed.

"See which way I'm spinning it?"

With the ball resting on his left index finger, Pete was "fanning" the ball and making it spin to the left. Typically, a person spins it left to right as the ball is fanned from the right, but Pete was spinning it in the opposite direction.

"I fan it backwards. I'm not sure why, but it's easier for me that way.

After a few hours of taking notes and recording Pete's thoughts, Pete invited us to stay for dinner. He enthusiastically prepared food for us. I knew the meal had to be healthy because that's the only kind of food that Pete allowed in the house.

There were no snacks or processed sugar to be found. I had been hooked on Dr. Pepper for years, and sugar and processed food was the norm for me. In Pete's house I had to put that out of my mind.

"Do you like lentil soup?"

"Never had it. Never heard of it."

"Serious? This is the best," Pete replied with pride.

I looked in the pot as Pete stirred. Then I noticed that the large pot of lentil beans was the only thing cooking. Later, we all sat at the dining room table and ate bowls of soup. It was delicious, but I had a hard time believing his kids or even his wife were actually enjoying this kind of meal. Where was the crawfish étouffée? The gumbo? Muffalettas? Red beans and rice? We were deep in the heart of Louisiana and Cajun country and the menu didn't fit my preconception. I realized that I had entered a huge part of Pete's world that was important to him—healthy eating.

"Eating like this will keep you alive," he advised me. "We really watch what we put in our bodies so I can be around a long time for my kids."

After the delicious dinner it was Pete's desire to give me a car tour of Covington. We walked out the back door and in the driveway sat a Chevy Caprice Classic and a Mercedes station wagon.

"The station wagon is my wife's," Pete explained. "Let's take the Caprice."

"Whoa. What's that?" I asked as I noticed a midnight blue sports car sitting in the yard.

"It's a Porsche. I stripped out every inch of it. Reupholstered; all new wood trim. It's like new."

34

I looked in the car and sat behind the wheel. I imagined driving up the Pacific Coast Highway in "Pistol Pete's" sports car. Yes, it was an awesome car, but more important to me, it was *his* car. I had no idea how much money he wanted for it, but I was already trying to put together my speech for my wife as to why I had to drive back to L.A. instead of flying.

"I'll take nine thousand cash," Pete casually offered.

"Nine thousand?"

"I need to get rid of it," Pete explained, "This is the car I almost killed myself in. I was so depressed."

"What do you mean?'"

"I thought about crashing it while I was speeding across the causeway bridge one night. All I ever knew since I was a little kid was playing basketball and I didn't know what to do with myself. I told a reporter one time that I didn't want to play ten years in the NBA, retire at thirty and die at forty! I wanted a championship ring more than anything in my life. I wanted to push the game to its limits and be part of a championship team. When I walked away, it nearly killed me."

"You were in Boston when you left the game, right?"

"Right. It was my last year. I was afraid the coach wasn't going to use me. I don't think he cared for me much. Reporters and people around the league were saying I didn't have much left after my knee injury and some said that I was done."

"I saw you shooting in L.A. You can still shoot better than most point guards in the league!" I boasted for him.

"You may be right," he laughed. "When they started saying things about me and my knee, I imagined it was like taking a feather pillow to the top of the Empire State Building and shaking out all the feathers. Imagine how the wind would blow those feathers all over the Big Apple."

35

"I've been up there. I know what you mean."

"That's how the rumors were floating around. Somebody said something about my knee and the rumor mill spread all over the league. There wasn't a chance of getting all those feathers back in the pillow."

We got into Pete's Chevrolet Caprice, which was a far cry from climbing into a customized Porsche. Pete put on his sunglasses, clicked his seatbelt buckle in place, adjusted his rear view mirror and started the car.

"Not exactly a chick magnet," I told Pete with a, smile as I referred to the conservative car he was driving.

"Those days are long over."

Pete put the car in gear and we rolled away from the quaint Victorian home. He seemed a bit out of place to me sitting behind the wheel.

"I do kinda feel like an old grandpa driving this car. My teammates would've given me a hard time about this ride, but I like it because I feel incognito."

"This fits you," I kidded. "You're retired."

"You can dish it out pretty good for a soap opera writer. They teach you that on *Days of our Lives*?"

I smiled, trying to grasp the reality that I was riding in a car with Pistol Pete Maravich, and I was also starting to realize that we were quickly becoming friends. It was my understanding that the NBA legend didn't let many people into his personal world, but for some reason he was graciously opening his heart and memories to me—often without any prompting.

"Did you know my dad's name is Peter? Peter Maravich?"

That would mean Pete was actually Pete Maravich Junior, I pondered.

"I thought your dad's name was 'Press?'"

"That's how most people know him, but that's a nickname. When my dad was a boy in Aliquippa, Pennsylvania, he delivered the *Pittsburgh Press* morning newspaper."

"Tell me about him," I suggested casually.

"You have to meet my dad. I can tell you about him, but until you meet him you won't really understand the man. I mean, if I told you that my father turned me into his little basketball android, that comes off kind of negative, but if I tell you that my dad inspired me and trained me to be the best athlete I could possibly become, then you would admire him. Plus, he's a basketball genius."

"Where is he? I gotta meet him."

"Pop has a place in Clearwater, Florida near our condo. We could go down there and spend some time with him if you want. He'll talk your ear off."

"That's what I want. Set it up."

I could tell that Pete was eager for me to meet his dad but at the same time he was anxious to start dumping stories on me about his somewhat famous father. For years I had read or known of the stories of "Pistol Pete" and his dad, Press. They had become one of the most famous coach-player duos in the history of basketball. Although they never made it to a championship, they had become legends in the United States with their exploits on the college court. What I didn't know was where it all started. I didn't know about Press Maravich and his time spent in the early professional league riding around in an old car with four other players.

"Pops was called the 'point-a-minute-man.' There's a sports page somewhere with that headline. I'll show you. It says, 'Press Maravich: The Point a Minute Man,' or something like that."

I had heard a lot about Press as a coach, but as Pete described his dad to me, I was interested to know everything I could about Press Maravich the player.

"My dad was a shooter and when you meet him you'll see that his mind is consumed with basketball knowledge. He's like a walking encyclopedia of basketball. He can tell you about some of the first great professional players like Dutch Denhert because he played against them or with them."

"Where did he get his start?

"Dad lived in Aliquippa, Pennsylvania. He'll tell you that all he ever wanted to do was to get out of that town. All his friends were destined to work the steel mills and to stay in the cold of Aliquippa. As a boy, my dad delivered newspapers for the *Pittsburgh Press*. That's how he got his name, *Press*. I think the kids teased him about always thinking that he knew everything. Dad was a ring leader and becoming a coach was a natural thing for him to do."

"What's his real name; full name, I mean?

"Peter. Peter Maravich."

"And, you're Peter Maravich Junior?"

"Yes."

"But you have an older brother. Why wasn't he the junior?"

"There's a story behind that, too. Ask my dad."

We walked down the hall of the mall later that day and at the time Pete Maravich was the most famous sports star that I'd ever spent time with in public. I must say it's a cool feeling to be walking with a beloved celebrity. For actors, politicians or professional athletes, strolling in public is often an adventure that they would rather avoid, but it was different with a retired star.

38

Guys like Pete survive the craziness of fame and then they ultimately get to relax in their retirement and become almost average citizens again. I recall the day I was in Matt Williams' office at Walt Disney, listening to a one-sided conversation. Matt had become a huge success creating and producing situation comedies, and he had seen unknown talent quickly become rich and famous. As Matt rose to the top of the TV industry, he hired me to join him at Disney and become part of his new production company, Wind Dancer. On this particular day, Matt was on the phone with a comedian who at the time was not a household name.

"This time next week you won't be able to go to Ralph's Supermarket to buy diapers for your baby," Matt looked at me and nodded. "Trust me, your life is about to change." Matt hung up the phone. He had been speaking with Tim Allen just before the premiere of *Home Improvement* was broadcast for the first time. Entertainers work hard for years and aren't recognized by anyone, but when fame arrives, privacy evaporates overnight. People might think that fame happened instantly for Tim, but like "Pistol Pete," Tim Allen had worked extremely hard to get his moment in the limelight.

"It was wild. I was a millionaire. I had honorary admiral status in the Navy. I had the money and fame and all that comes with it," Pete continued.

Pete was also collegiate basketball's all-time leading scorer, and as I write this book, he still is NCAA's leading scorer! Remember, he was averaging forty-four points a game before the three-point line existed. The 741 points he scored as a freshman didn't even count back in the 1960s because freshmen were not eligible to play varsity basketball.

The Louisiana State University basketball team record was three wins and twenty-three losses the year before the Maraviches showed up. "Pistol Pete" and his freshman Tiger teammates, known as the "Baby Bengals," played to sold out arenas as they racked up a 17-1 record. Of course, all Pete could think about after that year of "Showtime" fame and accolades was the one painful loss to Tennessee.

"They didn't let us play on the varsity when we were freshman," Pete explained.

"LSU fans must've been pretty excited to see who was coming up from the freshman squad," I replied.

"Oh, yes. Every freshman game, there was a huge line of people trying to get into the old Cow Palace."

"Why did they call it the Cow Palace?"

Not being from the South or from Louisiana, that part of the legend I didn't know.

"They had cows in there a lot. Rodeos and stuff. They would come in and put down a basketball court over the dirt for our games."

I looked at Pete wondering if he was pulling my leg, as he would so often do.

"We were seventeen and one my freshman year. I scored over fifty points six times and one game I had sixty-six. I missed the back end of two free throws at the end of the game. Darrel, I can shoot free throws blind folded, but that ball rolled around the rim and dropped to the floor. I couldn't believe it! We lost 75 to 73. I walked out the back door of the gym and I got lost for a few hours. I was so upset. I had let down my team, my school and the fans. I hated to lose. Because I had been programmed in my basketball android mind to win, losing made me feel horrible, and it also made me feel like I was always to blame."

40

Pete recounted the story as if it had happened the night before.

"I was thinking that it didn't matter if I was double and triple-teamed all night long. I should've helped my team win the game," Pete added.

As we walked down the hallway of a shopping mall, Pete adjusted his aviator sunglasses. I noticed almost everyone who passed us would glance or stare at Pete. People whispered and some pointed. A few passersby would say things such as, "Hey, Pistol!" or, "'Pistol Pete!"

Pete would nod and return a closed-lip smile.

"You do realize those dark glasses inside this building are not disguising who you are" I kidded, "You're six-five and you have floppy hair. The only thing missing is your saggy socks and a number forty-four on your T-shirt."

Pete laughed.

"You do know that you're "Pistol Pete," right?" I joked.

"You need to meet the first guy named Peter Maravich. When you talk to my dad you'll see how I got to this place in my life."

"I can't wait."

Our next stop was the Tampa, Florida airport. It was time to meet the man behind the legend.

CHAPTER 5

The Original Peter Maravich

"I was the only survivor of ten children," Press Maravich told me, as he looked me in the eyes. His face was kind and older now but I could tell that this man at one time had the looks of a 1940s movie star. He must have resembled a young William Holden or even a Kirk Douglas; with his strong-jaw and electric smile. Press had turn-on-a-dime expressions that would go from happy smiles to frightening frowns as he made a cogent point that should not be missed.

I faded away in my thoughts for just a moment as I let his words sink in. He had lost every brother and sister in his family? What a tragic beginning to life. He was a lone survivor. My father was the same age as Press, and the first time Press and I met, he reminded me of my father. My dad had suffered through the Great Depression and experienced heartache including the loss of his brother in battle. All my life, I recall my dad telling me how his brother's death in Normandy left a huge vacuum in his life.

"Just put me in a gunny-sack and throw me in a hole when I die. That's what they did to your Uncle Freeman," Dad would say as he choked back his emotions.

I couldn't imagine the heavy burden of injustice that Press must have felt when all of his siblings were wiped out by disease. No one from his immediate family was left in Press's young life. In fact, he had almost always been with without his biological parents. As I pondered the sad childhood of the legendary sports icon, I felt honored that I was privileged to meet him and hear about his past.

I felt blessed to get the precious time to hear his words of wisdom as if I had climbed to my own personal mountaintop to find the wise old sage.

I traveled from Los Angeles to Tampa, Florida, with one thing in mind. I had to record everything I could glean from the mind of this basketball master. I wanted to know how a guy from the steel mill town of Aliquippa, Pennsylvania, had survived the rough upbringing of the Great Depression, and chose a path in a fledgling professional sport to become one of the most revered minds of the game.

That may sound like hyperbole to some, but after hearing what people like John Wooden and others had said about the mind of Press Maravich, I knew there was much more to this man than most fans of basketball knew.

"Everything we had was because of the jobs we held at the Jones and Laughlin steel mill. When you were a kid in Aliquippa, that's where everyone figured they would end up and work for their entire life," Press reminisced as he leaned back into his easy chair. The wheels turned in his head as he recalled events six decades earlier.

"All the boys followed their dads into the same line of work. At the mills we had the rod mill, the carpenter shop, the tin mill or maybe the open hearth. That's what all our futures looked like to us. And most of my buddies were resigned to that notion of doing what their family members had done for work. But when I watched those trains pull out of the station and roll out of town, all I could think of was how much I wanted to be on one of those rail cars so I could escape to see the world."

What a strange moment it was for me. I had never met a man who reminded me so much of my own father.

"Let me tell you about my father," Press continued.

He had my attention. We instantly connected as I listened to not just his words, but also the rhythm and the inflection of them. I wondered if Press mesmerized me due to my heightened respect for warriors of his "greatest generation." Or, perhaps I had been pre-conditioned to listen to this man due to the fact that he was the same age as my father and their stories had so many parallels.

"My father died before I knew him," Press told me with a strange foreboding in his voice. "It's a terrible thing to grow up without your father."

The senior Maravich had been tragically killed in the wee hours of the morning while working near the tracks of a steel mill railroad. A locomotive crushed him to death. Press had heard stories about his father that made him regret more that he never got to know him. His stepfather, George Kosanovich, served admirably as Press's dad growing up, but there was never the closeness that Press longed for.

"We didn't get along too well. My dream of being something more than a steel worker rubbed my stepdad the wrong way. I always imagined that my real father would have been supportive and would have pushed me to make something important of my life."

"So he just wanted you to stay in Aliquippa like everyone else?"

"Yes, but he did have one strange goal for my life that I couldn't really understand. You'll laugh."

"What was it?"

"Well, he wanted me to play music."

"I'm not laughing. I'm a drummer. That's one way I paid for my college; playing drums," I told Press. "What kind of music did your stepdad want you to play?"

44

"Serbian songs from the old country," Press rolled his eyes.

I looked at Press, admiring his chiseled jaw and full head of thick hair. "You have a good look for the stage."

Press laughed, "This mug would scare people."

"I'm trying to understand why your step-dad would want you to play music? You wanted to be an athlete, but he was pushing music. Why?" I asked.

"So he could sing!" Press replied as if I should have known. "He and his cousins had a group called 'The Four Tons.' They were all giant guys who could sing and keep singing sometimes into the middle of the night! They would drink wine and eat Serbian foods until the women would finally scold them and make them stop. My stepdad wanted me to learn to play an instrument to accompany them."

"Like what? The piano?"

"Oh, he would've liked that. Actually, I might have liked that. First it was the banjo. Some salesman came by the house selling banjos and banjo lessons. If I took a year of lessons, I would get to keep the banjo. It was the company's way of pushing their instruments, I guess."

"How did that go?"

"It was stupid. I hated it. I took a year of banjo lessons, then a year of violin lessons and then, would you believe it? Harp lessons?"

"Harp lessons?"

"Yes! Like I was going to be a harp-playing angel or something," Press laughed and shook his head.

"That's about the time I got my nickname. I was carrying my violin home from a lesson one day, trying to avoid anyone seeing me."

"There's no shame in playing the violin."

45

"You weren't carrying it! I walked by a little shack that my stepbrothers had made, and I hid the violin case so I wouldn't have to hear them razz me about it. They were playing cards and shooting the breeze about this, that, and the other thing, and I would chime in like I knew everything. Whatever the subject, I would always jump into the conversation like I was an expert on the subject. My stepbrother got angry with me and shouted, '*I guess if you want to know anything, just ask the Pittsburgh Press!*'"

"Ah. So that's how you got your name?"

"Yes. The second I heard it, I thought, *that's a good nickname. Press Maravich. That's who I'll be.*"

Press and I visited for several hours that first day in Tampa. The trip to meet Press had been a long one for me, from one end of the United States to the other, but it was worth every moment. He was full of all kinds of stories, and since I was a lover of history, I vividly pictured his tales of historic times in America. He could talk endlessly about life in Pennsylvania, the WWII years, and his favorite topic, basketball—specifically Pete and basketball.

Press was more than willing to take me back to a different time and paint wonderful word pictures so I could get a better understanding of his childhood. I urged Press to keep delving into stories about his boyhood although I was yearning to hear his stories about WII and stories about his playing and coaching days.

"I loved basketball when I was a kid. We didn't have a basketball, so I would take some of my leftover *Pittsburgh Press* newspapers and wad them tight into a ball."

"How did you hold the paper together?"

"I'd wrap and smash the paper and then I got some kind of tape—whatever I could find—and I'd wrap it around that paper as tight as possible. That ball of paper was the only ball we had. Remember, we were all poor in the neighborhood, so we just had to make do."

"What about a basketball goal?"

"A light pole on the street."

"You'd just fasten a rim to a light pole?"

"Rim? We wished we had a rim. We had a bushel basket. It's like those stories about James Naismith out in Kansas. Coach Naismith was looking for an indoor sport for his physical education class and he mounted a peach basket at each end of the wooden gymnasium floor. That's how basketball was invented, you know. We look back now and just act like basketball has always been with us, but gymnasiums were for other sports back in the day. Anyway, we put that basket on the pole and I remember some of those old cold nights in Aliquippa, we would be out there in the snow and ten degree weather shooting and forgetting about homework and being indoors. That's how I started loving the sport."

Pete's condo was on the Gulf shore in Clearwater. The high-rise building offered spectacular views of the Gulf waters and endless horizon. That afternoon I discovered something that lots of Floridians know very well; lightning and rain show up every day. We took a short break, and as Pete cornered Press for a private chat in the kitchen, I walked to the sliding glass door and watched the bolts of lightning streak out of the dark clouds and into the deep water. On the beach a constant roar of a bulldozer pushing piles of sand filled the air.

The annoying beep, beep, beep of the dozer backing up began to irritate me because as I played back my interview tape. There was nothing I could do about it.

47

I glanced back into the kitchen where Press and Pete were speaking in hushed tones. The conversation in the kitchen seemed serious. There they were, father and son, but now the son seemed to tower high above his legendary father. Not as in height, but as in authority as if the son were giving advice to the father.

Out of all the photographs I had seen in *Sports Illustrated* and other publications, this wasn't a composition I had in my mind. Something was wrong. I could tell by the body language. I couldn't pry. It was personal. The conversation was intense but quiet. I noticed Press rubbing his shoulder and rolling it as if to show Pete that there was some range of motion, but from the wince on Press's face, there was also pain.

Pete didn't act like a man who had just been given bad news. He suggested that we go to a favorite diner of his that was across the bridge into Tampa.

"You guys can get some burgers and fries if you want. They have a veggie burger for me."

"Let's get outta here," Press smiled.

Pete stopped.

"Did you see the bedroom, Darrel? It gives me the creeps sometimes."

I'm sure the expression on my face was all he needed to continue the story. I looked back through the opened door and into the bedroom where I saw the bed and the layout of the room.

"One night I was sleeping in that bed. I woke up in a sweat and I saw standing at the end of the bed a huge, black figure. Right there," Pete pointed to the foot of the bed. "I couldn't make out a face. It was like Death in his hooded robe, but there was no face, just the pitch-dark figure of a being."

"It looked like a man?" I asked.

"It wasn't a man. It was a thing. I understood in that midnight hour what it means to 'taste fear.' There was immediately a strange taste in my mouth. That thing was here to kill me!"

The way Pete described it with such conviction sent chills down my back.

"The closer I get to God the more the enemy wants to destroy me. I was terrified from the top of my head to the tip of my toes. Wouldn't you be? That weird taste in my mouth was the taste of fear. I just looked at … that thing … and I screamed, 'In the name of Jesus Christ and the blood He shed, go! Get out! Get out of here!"

"And did it go?"

"It vanished. Greater is He that is in me than he that is in the world,'" Pete quoted the Bible verse as he left the room.

I stood there for a second looking at the large bed covered in a beautiful comforter and pillow shams. The room, decorated in light colors, was the total opposite of foreboding or frightening. If I was directing a film and my art director was to design the room as an environment for a dark spirit, I would have to tell them that the brightly colored and inviting space was not the vision I had for a demonic visitation. But Pete Maravich had just described to me in detail the moment and the intensity of his fear. I will never forget that room.

As we rode the elevator, I took another moment to realize where I was and what I was experiencing. Pistol Pete Maravich and his father, Peter "Press" Maravich were living legends and they were telling me their story.

I whispered to Frank, "This isn't a movie about Pete's childhood. There's too much here. I keep thinking we have a book."

"That's a great idea!" Frank said. "You should write a book and then we can base the film on the book."

"Part of the book," I added. "If this keeps up, this will be too much for a feature film. A mini-series, maybe," I explained.

A book? What was I thinking? Not only had I never written a feature film before, I had certainly never written someone's autobiography. And this was no ordinary autobiography. It would be the account of a person whose life I thought I knew through TV interviews and sports articles. But after spending just a few hours with him at his house and then at his condo in Florida, I realized I knew almost nothing about the real man. I set the book idea aside for a while and tried to concentrate on the reason for the visit. I was in Florida to hear the backstory and history of Pete so I would know how to write a movie that we wanted to call *The Pistol.*

CHAPTER 6
Like Father, Like Son

We sat at the counter of the restaurant and I made sure I sat next to Press because I know instinctively that every good story begins by understanding as much of the back-story as possible. I spoke with familiarity as if I had known him for many years. Press felt the same way about me, and because he was so passionate about his life and basketball, our conversations were fun and lively.

At times I was intimidated by his knowledge, but being a history buff, I kept up as best I could as he spoke of eras and places. Press would lose me sometimes when he mentioned names of coaches and players in the game during the 1940s and 1950s. All the while he would remove paper napkins from the silver dispenser and with a pen in one hand he would scribble lines and letters onto the napkins.

"I met Helen in Pittsburgh. Glen Miller's band was playing. She was the hatcheck girl in the hotel that night and I couldn't believe my eyes when I saw her. You ever hear of a guy falling in love at first sight?"

"I've heard it happens," I laughed.

"Darrel, I'm talking about true love. Real love."

"Sounds like you were smitten."

"Oh, yeah. God knew that Helen and I were supposed to be together. Pete's mother was a real beauty. I never loved any woman more than I loved Helen, and when she passed away I never wanted anyone else."

The room grew quiet as we continued eating. Press didn't have to tell me he was living with the sweetness of his memories of Helen as well as the sting of how she died.

"She was the most beautiful woman in the world," Press continued, "When she had her problems, I didn't know what to do. I wasn't home very much. I was trying to recruit new players and take care of Pete's little sister at the same time. Basically, I was trying to coach and keep my job."

Suddenly, I was lost in his story because Press would speak assuming that I knew more about his life saga than I actually did. The pain of living with the drama of Helen's alcoholism was the ghost in the life of Press that had never been put to rest.

"She would hide liquor bottles in shoes or drawers ... I even found a bottle in the chandelier. Helen took to drinking when I was gone. Honestly, basketball was like a mistress, taking my attention away from my sweet wife."

Pete interrupted Press and his feelings of overwhelming guilt.

"She was a great mom," Pete chimed in. "I only have good memories, really."

"We hid a lot from Pete and the other kids. They really didn't know much until later on. Helen drank until she took her life," Press remarked with sadness.

"It wasn't her, Pop. The alcohol made her into somebody else and that's the truth. That's what I believe."

Press pushed his plate away and continued scribbling onto a napkin. As much as I wanted to discover more about the past that destroyed her position in the family, I didn't want to drill down into the psychology or ramifications of chemical dependency.

I realized, however, that if we were to recreate the real story of an American sports legend and tell it with integrity, I would have to better understand the dynamics of Pete and his dad.

52

Before I met Pete and Press, I had a fantastic view of Pete and his world. As a screenwriter, I wanted to create an uplifting *Herbie the Love Bug* or a *Son of Flubber* kind of childhood story that would inspire and give the family film the innocent "heart" that Pete had requested. I didn't want to rip out hearts with deep emotional stories of Pete's tragedies.

Then it dawned on me. The American Dream has always taken on its own form. The dream depends on so many factors such as where one is born, or what worldview a person takes into adulthood. The book would be the proper format to tell much of the Maravich story.

I had to immediately force the cowardly thought of not being an author out of my head. I would become an author, I pledged to myself. I had earned an English degree! *I've been educated enough to put sentences and thoughts into a readable structure! Might as well put my knowledge and some acting to good use and pretend to know what I'm doing.* It was at that moment that I realized the acting skills I had been taught at the American Academy of Dramatic Arts would come in handy. *How hard can it be? I'm going to act like an author and act like I know how to write a book.*

The storytelling had taken a dark turn, and I began to hope that we could get back to laughing and talking about other things I might want to put in the movie. We were surrounded by 1950s decor in the diner that day and that was the time period in Pete's life that interested me the most. It was a time for adventure just before his legend would launch.

Together Press and Pete built their stories upon each other, and like bricklayers they threw down one memory on top of another. Brick-by-brick the stories would neatly pile upon each other.

The conversation between Pete and Press seemed to always move back to basketball whether they were sharing current or past events. It became clear that this duo possessed much more than a father and son relationship. They were coach and player for years and clearly the best of friends. Press was still a wise mentor and Pete was the student. If Miyagi and Daniel had been father and son in *The Karate Kid* movie, this is what it they might have looked like growing old. Press and Pete loved and respected each other deeply. They were living testimonies of what a father and son relationship should look like.

"What do you think of this one?" Press asked as he slid a napkin down the counter in front of Pete.

Pete studied a diagram that Press had been drawing on the flimsy paper. After a moment, Press grew frustrated.

"What? You don't get it?" Press pointed with the pen as he continued, "A forward passes in to the guard here as the other forward sets a pick here. If that guard's not open, the center busts through the lane and looks for the pass here. Maybe a layup or he pulls up for an eight-footer."

"It might work," Pete chewed his food.

"What? Are you kiddin'?" Press grunted, "Of course it would work. Why wouldn't it work?"

"It could work," Pete said.

"What's the problem?"

"I said it could work, Pop," Pete assured him.

"Ahhhhh," Press grunted as he tucked the napkin in his pocket and then pulled a fresh one from the napkin dispenser.

"Pops has a thousand in-bounds plays," Pete explained.

Press corrected, "Ten thousand."

"He's done this all my life. He sits around drawing plays. He used to have coaches come over to our house after games at Clemson or Davis-Elkins or wherever he was coaching. They would sit at the kitchen table and mom would serve coffee and cake."

"Helen would have to ask the other coaches to leave after a few hours," Press laughed, "Or she would go to bed and leave me and the guys talking all night."

"He's talking about the opposing coaches," Pete clarified.

"Yes. After games I had coaches from the other schools come over. We would talk strategies and plays. To me, it wasn't always about winning; it was about making the game better."

"It was about winning," Pete blurted.

"No. Not all the time. I liked helping other coaches," Press chimed back in.

At the time, I didn't know if that scene would make it into my movie, but I could just picture other coaches falling asleep at the table as Press kept dreaming on about what basketball could be. Press went on to explain how his quest was to elevate the play of basketball by teaching fundamentals to every player. It sounded simple, but to Press, fundamentals were never perfected by anyone.

The closest Press got to perfecting an athlete on the court was the education of his son. Pete was the child who was put into a groove for basketball success due to the knowledge and inspiration of his father.

Pete had a highly motivated college-tested basketball genius living in his house for all his formative years. Pete ate, slept and lived basketball and his father encouraged the child's basketball lifestyle.

Press confirmed to me the legend that young Pete slept with a basketball instead of a Teddy bear and his prayers at bedtime were about his becoming the greatest basketball player to ever live.

Pete began to reminisce: "I wrote an essay in junior high school for English class. I wrote about the dream I had for my life. I actually predicted that I would become a professional basketball player in the NBA and I wrote that my dream was to be the first player to make a million dollars. The third part to my dream was that I would win a big gold ring that proved to the world that I was one of the best players to ever play the game."

"You got the NBA contract and you were the first million-dollar player," Press chimed in proudly as he kept drawing another in-bounds play on the napkin.

"But I never got the ring," Pete said, as he paid the check and stood to leave, "That really doesn't matter anymore. DC, you'll be staying at Pop's place tonight. Frank can stay at my condo. That way you and Pop can keep talking and I can get some rest!" he smirked.

It was Pete's way of saying he needed to give his mind a rest from the memories.

"That sounds good," I replied, "I have a lot of questions for you, Coach."

"I can write it all down for you if you'd rather do it that way," Press said, always wanting to cut to the chase and keep things moving.

"I'll keep my recorder going and you just keep telling me what you want to tell me, if that's okay," I encouraged.

"Sounds good to me," Press replied, "but remember, your movie shouldn't be about me. It's got to be about "Pistol Pete," the greatest basketball player to ever play the game."

"Pop, just let him write what he wants to write," Pete tried to inject some humility.

"It's the truth. In my house, I raised the future of basketball. I mean, there was Bob Cousy, with his dribbling and shooting, but he was nothing like Pete. Pete had great fundamentals, great footwork, deceptive passing … between his legs … behind his back, going full speed down the court. Overhand passes. Under-hand full court passes. No-look left or right. Nobody had ever seen what Pete did and no one ever will."

"This is what you're in for, DC."

"It's true. He won't say it, but it's true," Press nodded.

Pete escorted us to his car and we headed back to the condo to get my luggage.

"He'll talk your ear off," Pete warned with a wry smile.

I nodded to Pete and told him that I was up to it. I was used to listening to stories of the past. I had spent dozens of hours with my father as he told me his stories of dancing the jitterbug in the 1920's, surviving The Great Depression and serving in the Army during WWII. I looked forward to a few hours alone with Captain Peter Press Maravich.

"Pete got me a place in Indian Shores. It's nice. We'll get you settled in and then I have lots to tell you. You know, Pete and John Wooden and I traveled to instruct at some basketball camps. I can tell you all about when I coached at Clemson and LSU. Oh, yeah, and remind me to tell you about the time I almost killed my navigator."

"Navigator?"

"I had a pretty good temper when I was a pilot during the war. But the guy deserved to be killed if you ask me. I'll tell you later. It's a good story."

I knew the night ahead would be memorable. My introduction to the world of Pistol Pete Maravich was becoming richer and more interesting because I had the privilege of meeting the original Peter Press Maravich. Press was a dreamer and an innovator. The story of "Pistol Pete" was astounding and sometimes unbelievable but as I began adding the tales that Press had to tell, Pete's life story became even more legendary.

CHAPTER 7
More Than a Movie

"It's bone cancer," Pete bowed his head. "Pop has been having a lot of soreness in his shoulder. I didn't think too much of it, but when he went to the doctor, they did tests and the cancer is definitely in the bone."

I was shocked at the news regarding the health of Press Maravich. The private discussion that Press and Pete had earlier—the quiet whispers in the kitchen, was the moment Press was revealing to his son that bone cancer had been discovered. Press had always been there for Pete from his cradle to that moment. Almost everything Pete knew in his life was because of the constant input and instruction that he had received from his father. Character, hard work, dedication, discipline, common sense, education and unconditional love were just some of the qualities that Pete acquired from a true American icon and hero—his dad.

"We'll fight this thing. We'll beat it. I'll do whatever we have to do to find the right doctors. We'll eat the right food … take the right medicines," Pete remarked in a private moment to me. "I'm not going to let him go without a fight, that's for sure. Pop's so tough; I don't think cancer will have a chance."

I could tell that as sure as Pete was, there was a hint that he was simply trying to convince himself that a cure for his dad rested in the future. Allowing his mind to think any different was not in Pete's nature. As he talked about his hero facing an uncertain future, I began projecting myself into his situation.

My father and Press were almost exactly the same age. They served in the same Army. They freed the world from the same tyranny. They loved God, country and family and would die for any of those affections. Personally, I would have been shattered had I just received devastating news such as that about my dad.

Later that night, I settled into Press's condo and we visited about his life and times as a coach and player and war hero. Press didn't bring up the subject of the cancer. I didn't want to push too hard for information with the news of his illness being so fresh, but Press was an open book. He would tell me if he wished.

Honestly, I wasn't sure if the intense drive to download his story to me that night was coming from his natural exuberance of life, or if the news of "terminal" cancer had become the reason for his wanting to tell me everything he could think of.

As I sat listening and recording his story, I had to put out of my mind that this new friend; this friendly, grandfatherly man, filled with a wealth of knowledge and experience had his impending death in the forefront of his thinking. As he shared stories from his past, there was no sign whatsoever that he was ill. He never rubbed his shoulder or complained about a thing. He was focused and clear-minded; wanting to dispense all the information he could to give me ideas for a movie or a book about his son.

"Pete was so mad at me when I told him I took a job at LSU," Press said, as he relived that moment. "I seriously thought he would run away, he was so angry."

"I'm sure he wanted to play in the Atlantic Coast Conference," I added.

"Pete always wanted to play in the Atlantic Coast Conference because of the basketball reputation and having grown up in South Carolina. The ACC teams were the ones he followed and wanted to play for. His ultimate dream was to play at North Carolina or Duke. What really made him mad was that I had signed with a university that had no reputation for basketball and was only known as a football school."

In the 1960s when Press was hired at Louisiana State University in Baton Rouge, the university was known as a national powerhouse in football. As the successful football program basked in light of extraordinary fan support and games were played in a monstrous stadium, the neglected basketball program was a second-tier affair. They were expected to always be lackluster and no fun to watch. Whether they won or not really didn't matter much to anyone. The basketball squad played in the Cow Palace. It was an old structure used for livestock shows and it was far cry from Pete's dream of playing for the North Carolina Tar Heels.

"I kinda threatened him," Press nodded. "I told him that it was LSU or nowhere. Pete was not a stellar student and a lot of Pete's fans today don't realize that after high school Pete spent a year in a military academy attempting to get his grades where they needed to be to attend college. The academy proved to be a nice preparatory stage. The year before entering LSU gave Pete a chance to grow both mentally and physically as he was forced to attend class and compelled to play a lot of basketball."

"I never knew that. I think most people just remember Pete going straight from high school to LSU," I replied curiously.

"No. He wasn't ready for college."

Press seemed irritated at that thought.

61

"TV wasn't like it is today. Heck, you rarely saw basketball on television. It's hard to believe with all the sports on TV these days. Anyway, I told Pete that if he came with me he would play. He and I could change the way LSU thought of and played basketball. With his style of play and some of my innovation, we could really make a difference. I told him we could turn LSU into a basketball university, too. I don't think he believed me, but of course he was still very angry about the whole situation."

"What made Pete give in?"

"It was tough. Pete was really mad. He yelled and told me that he would never play basketball at LSU. I probably shouldn't have said it, but I got in his face and told him if he didn't come with me, I would never speak to him again. He wouldn't be my son."

"Wow. How did he react?"

"He was furious. It was a terrible thing to say to a son, but I didn't want anyone else to coach Pete. I knew what he could be on the college level. I knew he could be the greatest ball-handler, passer and shooter the game had ever seen. I also knew I could help properly prepare him for the professional level. I hated to say what I said, but I had to threaten him to go with me. Back in the day, I had a pretty bad temper."

"Yes. Speaking of your temper … let's back up a little," I suggested. "After lunch today you said something about nearly killing your navigator. What was that about?"

"Oh, yeah, I could've killed him. I almost threw him out of my airplane at about eight thousand feet. No parachute and into the ocean," Press declared without a smile.

"You're serious?"

"Yes."

"I have to hear that story."

62

The look in his eyes made me wish to hear that story next. When I hear a story with the notion of translating it someday into a movie, I make notes as to what event evokes the most emotion and should be used in a screenplay. I could picture the old coach in front of me as a younger airman jettisoning a guy out a bomb bay door.

"I want to hear all the basketball stories, but the suspense is killing me. Can you tell me what happened to you during the war; especially the story about you and your navigator?" I asked.

"Sure. Well, you know, I never dreamed as a kid that I'd be fighting a war. Lots of our family fought in World War One. They called that the *Great War* or the *War to End All Wars*. Us kids just wanted to live our lives and get on with it, but after the Japanese bombed Pearl Harbor in Hawaii, that sealed it for us."

"Right. About that navigator?" I asked.

"Hold on. Let me tell this in order. I have a few more things to tell you before I get to nearly killing a man in my bomber," Press laughed. "Let me fill in the blanks and get to that because it'll be good for you to know where I came from."

I laughed and calmed my curiosity as I allowed him to tell me what he wished.

"Okay, I'll shut up. So you were a kid playing basketball in Aliquippa. Start there."

"For me, figuring a way out of the steel mills was first priority," Press continued. "I remember one time we were playing outside in the snow, shooting our make-shift basketball into that basket I told you about. It was late and up walked a preacher Reverend Anderson."

"Were you in trouble?"

"Nah. I wouldn't have cared anyway. We were out shooting baskets, not getting into mischief," Press defended himself. *Who's the leader of this group?* The reverend asked us. "I told him I was the leader. I was always the leader and the kids knew it."

Press continued, telling me that Reverend Anderson had come to make the kids an offer.

"The Reverend took me to his church's Sunday school building and showed me around. He suggested that I bring all my friends into the warm building to play basketball. I looked around the place and pointed out that there were no backboards or goals. *I'll get them ordered and put up for you boys,"* Anderson told us, *"but there is a condition. If I put up the goals, you'll come to a Bible class three times a week – an hour each day."*

"I thought it over and then I ran back to my buddies who were still playing out in the cold. I became the preacher. I preached a sermon to the boys about the virtues of playing indoors where the rain and snow wouldn't freeze our fingers and toes to the bone. *It's warm in that joint all the time!* I told the guys. *The reverend will get us real backboards, goals and nets and there's a wood floor. And Reverend Anderson says he'll buy us a new ball or two."*

He ended the story by saying that the boys agreed to attend the Bible studies in exchange for warm facilities.

Press took a sip of hot tea and then continued, "When we were kids, the professional teams in basketball were starting to form and they began traveling around. Men were becoming celebrities of the game. Guys like Dutch Dehnert, Joe Lapchick and Nat Holman were players that we read about and started admiring because they were making money doing what we loved to do just for fun."

"So, all the reverend asked was that you attend some Bible classes? How did that go?"

"After a few weeks of playing in the warm Sunday school building and studying the Bible with the reverend, names like Moses, Daniel and Noah became as familiar as Dutch, Joe and Nat."

Press thought for a moment and then skipped a few years to his high school days.

"All I remember about my high school days is how hard I worked. I mean, on and off the basketball court. I went to school. I was the captain of my high school basketball team my junior and senior years and Coach Lippe liked the way I took charge of the team. At the same time, I was working as a pipe threader in the mill, and to be honest, I can hardly remember sleeping during my sophomore, junior and senior years in high school."

"No kidding. You must've been pretty good in high school to endure all the steel mill work as well as the hard work on the court."

"I loved it. I worked on my skills all the time. Remember, basketball was my ticket out of town. I wanted to be a professional basketball player and make money playing and traveling the country. That's what drove me every day of my life."

I wasn't up on my basketball history at the time of my interview with Press so I unashamedly asked, "Was there much professional basketball going on when you finished high school?"

"Well, sure, but you can't compare it to anything today, or like when Pete was playing pro ball. I mean, it was the thirties and the Great Depression was still going on."

"Do you remember when basketball started to get some traction as a sport?" I asked.

The new indoor sport was so popular that it really caught fire across the country. The people creating basketball teams started the American Basketball League and the schedules they played weren't real structured yet. Probably the Original Celtics were the only white team with a regular game schedule that included lots of travel. There were a couple of African American teams like the Harlem Globetrotters and the New York Rens, but they had to stay in the northern states and they didn't have much money to travel."

"When did you get your shot at professional ball?" I asked.

Press thought for a moment and then answered, "It was when I was known as Munnell?"

"What's that mean?"

"The name I used. I changed my name to 'Munnell.'"

I sat up in my chair; afraid I was getting sleepy and perhaps misunderstanding Press. It had been a long day.

"Oh. Okay. Hold on. Why would you change your name to Munnell?"

"I was still in high school so I couldn't play on a pro team or I would lose my eligibility."

"Oh, I get it."

"There was a team out of Ambridge, Pennsylvania that saw me playing high school ball. They needed a shooter and ball-handler like me, so they asked me to play in tournaments with them on the weekends."

"That's the first time you got paid to play?"

"Nothing to get excited about. Ten bucks a game, but it was money and I wasn't sweating it out in a steel mill to earn it. Plus, I got a lot of experience."

66

"Were you playing professionally when you played in college?"

"Yes."

"How did you pull that off?"

"I did what I had to do to get to where I wanted to be, you know?" Press answered unapologetically.

"Where did you go to college?"

"Davis and Elkins."

"I'm not familiar."

"If I'd gone to Duke, you would've known that team, eh? That's where I wanted to go. Duke made me an offer to play, but back then there were no full-ride scholarships and the partial one they offered me wasn't enough. I was poor!"

"Did you receive a lot of offers?"

"I got plenty. I thought about going to Long Island University, because I had heard a lot about their coach, Clair Bee."

Clair Bee was an innovative coach whose books influenced Press. Press had read that Coach Bee would sit and discuss basketball with other coaches and was considered one of the great minds in the game. Press also got an offer from Duquesne, but one of Press's reasons for playing basketball and attending college was so he could get far away from Aliquippa or Pittsburgh. Going to a Pittsburgh University like Duquesne didn't line up with his dream.

"Davis and Elkins was my choice. It's a small college in Elkins, West Virginia. One of my best friends decided to go there, so that helped my decision. At D & E, I played four seasons and one of those years I was one of the top scorers in the nation."

It was at that small college where Press signed up for a United States Naval Reserve Air Corp flight-training course. Press excelled in his training to become a pilot.

"After I graduated with my business degree and a pilot's license, I was a bit depressed when I realized that the only job I could get quickly was back in Aliquippa working as a pipe-threader at Seamless Tube."

When the fall came that year, Press joined the Clarksburg Pure Oilers out of West Virginia and began playing weekend tournaments. One weekend, the Oilers were matched against the World Champion Detroit Eagles. Press's childhood hero, Dutch Denhert of the Original Celtics, coached the Eagles. Dutch was a super-star player who transitioned into a coach. He enjoyed immense popularity playing for the Celtics.

Press had dreamed of meeting his idol someday in the future and that day turned out to be the same day Press scored thirty against Coach Dehnert's Eagles. After the game Coach Denhert met up with Press and asked him to join the Eagles for the rest of the season.

"We played seventy-five games and I made money doing what I dreamed of doing. You think the games are getting physical these days? I got patched up after every game back then. Fans came to see rough and tumble play. We got black eyes, lost teeth and someone was always receiving stitches somewhere on their head or face," Press explained. "You've heard of 'cagers?' That was us! We played in cages. Chicken wire was stretched around the edge of the court to keep the ball in and the fans off the floor."

"Were you playing mainly in the Northern U.S., like the old teams?

"Nah, we played all over. Ever heard of Abe Saperstein?

"The Globetrotters?"

"Yes, the guy who created the Harlem Globetrotters. Now, that guy had a business mind and when I was playing he was the traveling secretary for our team, the Detroit Eagles. He knew how to get folks out to the games and how to get us from one place to the next. There were several teams traveling the U.S. in those big ole black cars. We'd all pile in and drive for hundreds of miles at a time. One night, all the guys were bone tired so I said I would drive. The problem with that plan was that I didn't know how to drive."

"How did that go?"

"In the dead of the night, all the guys were asleep when a cow walked out on the road in front of me. I smashed into that crazy thing and mashed up the front of the team car. I turned around to check on the guys and that accident didn't wake up one of them. Next morning, when the boss saw the damage on the car, I lied and told him it must've happened in the parking lot before we left. I told you I was a talker. He bought my story."

"You said you played seventy-five games. Was that a season?"

"It was a season for me," Press remarked as he shook his head. "We showed up in New Orleans and checked in to our hotel late one night. Before long there was a telegram at the front desk waiting for me."

"What year was this?" I asked with a hunch.

"Nineteen-forty-one."

"Ah, I see where this is going.

"When I took flight training from the U.S. Navy, I also signed the line that said they could call me up to serve if my country needed me."

69

"That would sure be another way to escape the steel mills," I kidded.

"For sure. I reported to Anacostia Naval Air Station for aviator training and before I knew it I was told to report to the commander's office. I had no idea what was coming next, but I soon found out that I was summoned because he knew I was a professional basketball player and he wanted me to coach a team to go up against what he called, the alphabet teams."

"What's an alphabet team?"

"C.I.A. (Central Intelligence Agency), F.B.I. (Federal Bureau of Investigation)."

Press asked if I was getting tired of his stories and I told him I was in his condo to listen if he wanted to talk all night. I had my tape recorder going and plugged into the wall. As I watched Press stand, walk and navigate around his home, I could imagine this older man as a young "baller." Since my little league days when my dad was my coach, coaches have been like father figures to me. Perhaps that is why I often use the names of my real-life coaches when I'm creating characters in film and television scripts.

In my first movie, *The Pistol: The Birth of a Legend*, the coach is named Coach Pendleton. In real life Coach Tom Pendleton taught me about perseverance and making the best of my situation because I was usually the smallest kid on the team. He pushed me to try harder and train more in order to compete. I am convinced that he kept me off the football field because he didn't want me to get killed! In the springtime he was my track coach who transitioned me from a sprinter into a long-distance runner using seven and eight-mile workouts each afternoon after school.

Maybe that was the visceral reaction I felt that night sitting in Press Maravich's living room. He was so much like my mentors in high school sports. But more than that, he reminded me a lot of my father. Having a father who speaks into your dreams, teaches you things, and shares his life experiences is the greatest gift a son will ever know. My heart aches for children who have no father or mother to coach and mentor them.

Press walked across the room, reached into a bedroom and flipped on the light switch.

"You'll sleep in here."

"Thanks, Coach."

"Call me 'Press,'" he replied as he tugged on the bed-spread.

"I wrote a book called *Two Minutes of Basketball*," Press said as he adjusted his glasses. "I'll give it to you if you promise me you'll rewrite it."

"You want me to get your book published?"

"And put Pete's name on it."

I smiled, thinking he was joking.

"I have it in my files. It's yours."

"Actually, it sounds like it's yours! That's an interesting business proposition, Press. What's it about?"

"It has little sayings or thoughts to inspire a young player. It could be for an older player too. It's like doing your exercises in the morning. You read a little chapter; should take you two minutes to get through it all. A kid reads it and locks it in their thoughts and then they ponder it through the day."

"Like an inspirational book. I have some of those that have quotes of the day. Something like that?" I asked.

71

"Yes. But it's about basketball. People are so busy these days and some folks don't even take time to read anything, but a kid who wants to get better and be the best player he can be will like reading it."

"Okay, but I don't think we should put Pete's name on it as the author. You wrote the book."

"Pete's famous! I'm not. People love him. If it has his name on it more kids will see it and want to read it. More moms and dads will buy the book. 'Pistol Pete's Two Minutes of Basketball.'"

Press left as I walked into the guest room for a moment. I looked into the dresser mirror and thought of how many of my friends would have done anything to spend five minutes with Press or Pete. The confidence I heard in his voice was the same confidence I had heard from my father all my life. When men of virtue speak with confidence, there is an innate desire to not only listen but to learn. I wanted to know what Press knew about life.

Then it dawned on me. Press never told me the navigator story!

CHAPTER 8
Press Unleashed

When I returned to the living room, Press was rifling through papers. Many of his personal papers from decades of coaching and scouting were typed notes. Hundreds of others were pages of his handwritten notes. The only thing all the scribbles, scratches and thoughts on paper had in common was basketball.

"Coach John Wooden and I took Pete with us to Israel one year to coach at a basketball camp," Press said.

"Yes, you mentioned that earlier. Are you guys still close?"

"Pretty good friends. Pete was always the star of the show when we did the camps. You should've seen the students when Pete came on the court dribbling and shooting. They had never seen anything like it and they've never seen anything like it since, I'll guarantee that. Darrel, I still get angry when I hear someone use the word 'cocky' or 'showboat' when they talk about Pete playing ball. 'Hot dog!' Yeah, that's the one they used the most."

"I remember reading about the poster some 'Pistol Pete' haters made that asked, 'Why are hot dogs twenty-five cents in Philadelphia and a million dollars in Atlanta?'"

"Just because Pete could dribble through other player's legs and then his own legs and then pull up for an off-balance one-handed fade away didn't make him a hotdog. Just because his fundamentals had flare didn't make him a 'hot dog.' It made him the greatest offensive basketball player anyone had ever seen. Fundamentals were what I stressed. That's what all the drills I created were about."

73

When Press looked me in the eyes and made that dec-laration regarding his son there was no hedging. There was no tempering of the statement. This iconic coach of the 1960s and 1970s believed without a doubt that he had raised, trained, mentored and coached the greatest basketball player to ever play high school, college and professional basketball.

"Basketball was everything to me. I could see what it could be in the future if coaches and players would focus on being the best they could possibly be," Press continued, "but pushing the game to the limits would have to be done by those who perfected their skills. Dribbling behind the back or through your legs is an efficient way to change directions; it's not about being flashy. But you wanted to hear about my time in the war ..."

"I want to hear whatever you have to say."

"I flew my airplane like I played ball. Fearlessly. Be-fore I got shipped out to the Pacific I remember flying over D.C. I saw a prison down below me and the inmates were out in the exercise yard. I buzzed that yard and did a few maneu-vers that had them all waving and cheering for me!"

"You were a showman."

"Too much of one. When I landed back at the base my commander walked up to me with a shovel and a pick. I asked what the tools were for and he reminded me that the plane I was flying had big numbers on the side that were easy to iden-tify."

"Someone at the prison called the base."

"Right. My punishment was digging a six-by-six foot hole for no reason other than to serve as a reminder to respect and conform."

"My dad ended up in Europe during the war. Where were you?" I asked.

"Well, I went to San Diego for more training and one day the chief petty officer walked up with a clipboard and asked, 'South Pacific or Alaska?' I figured it was too cold in Alaska but hot in the South Pacific. I flipped a coin and I was off to the Hawaiian Islands."

"So was basketball over for a while?"

"No! You know, just like what happened to me in D.C., I was given the job to coach our basketball team on Oahu Island, and we even won the island championship. Basketball would find me because of my reputation, but really, I would find it too. If I saw a goal and a ball, I got the same feeling I did when I was a kid in Aliquippa. I just had to play."

"Did you run across any of the other professional players who enlisted?"

"Not that I can remember, but I made a best friend on the island who was an All-American basketball player. Herbie Bonn was his name," Press recalled. "He played at Duquesne and grew up around where I did so we really hit it off and shared lots of life stories."

Press took a sip of his tea and I could tell he was reliving that time in his mind. He put down his cup and rubbed his shoulder for the first time that evening.

"Shall we call it a night, Press?"

Press responded in an unexpected way, "I'm okay. You know napalm? Heard of it?"

"Sure. They used napalm bombs to clear the jungles in Vietnam. Right?"

Napalm was a bomb consisting of a gel mixture. When dropped on a target the ordinance is actually a firebomb with a fuel gel that causes it to stick to whatever it touches. When it meets its target, the effect of the five thousand degree flames wipes out nearly everything.

75

"Like I said, Herbie and I really hit it off because we both loved basketball and we were from the same state and all. That night after we won the island basketball championship we got orders and they told us our planes would be carrying a new ordinance. It was napalm.

"Herbie was in his plane and I was in mine as we both taxied to the runway for takeoff. Herbie was on the radio, still talking about the game and about how we would celebrate when we got back to the island. We joked and I remember he kept calling me 'Coach.' I told him we'd go out later and knock back a few, even if this run took us all night. Herbie said, *After you.* I told him that he had played great and that we wouldn't have won the championship without him. I said, *After you, my friend.*"

Press stared at his feet and stopped recounting the story. From the look on his face, I was certain that the rest of the events he would recall would not be happy ones.

The awkward silence reminded me of the times when I would sit with my father and listen to his war stories. He would come to a particularly horrible memory and his words would falter. I was getting the same feeling as I watched Press stare into the distance. Just like I would do with my father, I sat in silence and let him speak when ready to continue.

"Herbie's plane ..."

Press took another drink of his tea and he swallowed hard enough for me to hear it.

"His plane reached the end of the runway and it just became a terrible ball of fire," Press recounted as he ran his wrist under his nose and looked away.

"I'm sorry, Press."

Press cleared his throat a few times and sat silently.

Finally, Press continued. "We were so proud to be from Pittsburgh and to be fighting for our country. All of us guys from the steel mills of PA, we had a lot of pride. Basketball glued us together."

I didn't dare interject as Press was at such an emotional part of his story.

Finally, Press continued, "Even my crew on our bomber was like a team. Everybody had his specialty. Herbie was a heck-of-a pilot and an All-American ballplayer. It's hard. Real hard."

I couldn't help but think that these "iron men" of the greatest generation were simply put together in a different way than men of my generation. They were children during the Great Depression when food and necessities of life were often luxuries. Necessary things in life were not "expected things."

The only survivor left of eleven children, Press stood as a monument to perseverance. It was his inner grit that was on display as I listened. The heart and character of Coach Press Maravich was that of a champion.

"Everyone on Herbie's plane was killed in an instant in that napalm fireball. It's hard to get that moment out of my mind, so I try not to think about it. I wish Herbie could've lived. We would still be friends today. I know we would've been."

Press wiped a tear from his eye with the back of his hand and continued, "I parked my plane, against the commander's orders. I couldn't go up. Not after that. I stayed drunk for three days. Herbie was my best friend. I never had a friend like that and I've never had one like him since."

The war-hardened coach persevered and shared more stories about The Black Cats, the name of Press's bomber squadron.

Press described how he would fly dangerous and unpredictable night flights to destroy Japanese cargo ships trying to get military supplies to their troops. The ships became known as "midnight coffins" as Press and the Black Cats took them out during the squadron's nocturnal flights.

"Oh, I never told you about nearly killing that guy," Press remembered.

"I wasn't going to let you forget," I assured him.

"It all started off pretty bad. I got permission to head back to the mainland for some R & R in San Diego. I really needed it too. I was spending most of my life each day in a bomber. Fifteen months, hundreds of night runs and the death of Herbie had me worn down pretty bad," Press explained.

"Fifteen months of bombing raids would wear down anyone," I remarked.

"Just as I got to San Diego, they told me, *Cap, we're sending you back out.* What could I do? It's the military and they own you. I mean, that's why we were there. In a matter of hours I'm back in a B-17. The crew was made up of guys I had never met. It was like getting traded to a new basketball team full of players you've never seen before."

"Remember when you were a kid in Aliquippa, wanting to jump a train and see the world? I'll bet you never thought it would be like this," I reminded Press.

"We didn't dream of war. We dreamed of accomplishing things. War is the stupidest thing humans ever thought up. That's for sure. But, when bad people are doing things you have to protect your country," Press continued.

"Yes, sir."

"We climbed up out of San Diego and soon, rain began hitting the plane hard."

"Did you turn back?"

"We were getting knocked around so I radioed back to the tower that I wanted to get the aircraft and my guys back on the ground. They denied us and ordered me to stay the course. Yeah, about that time I was really wishing for good ole Aliquippa and simpler times."

"I bet."

"'Proceed to the destination,' they told me. Well, about eight hundred miles out over the ocean with clouds over us and a storm under us I told my radioman to ask permission one more time. They turned us down again. That really made me mad. So, I took that bird down to about two hundred feet off the water so I could see what I was really up against, but it didn't help. I was flying blind using just my altimeter to keep up out of the water."

"What was your crew thinking?"

"What do you mean?"

"You're flying just above the ocean during a rain storm. That couldn't have made them feel too good."

Press laughed, "Oh, yeah, they were a mess. They were all a bunch of green kids. I had been flying and doing bombing runs for over a year, so I guess I got to where I was never afraid. I'd get mad, but not afraid. Yes, I'd say my crew was pretty scared."

"How long did that last?"

"A couple hundred miles. It had to be over two hundred miles of flying with zero visibility. However long that would take. Then, all of a sudden we broke through the tail of the storm to find blue sky and sunshine. I was happy we hadn't run into an island or another plane. My crew cheered and clapped they were so relieved."

"Okay, so what led to you wanting to kill your navigator," I asked.

"I'm getting there. As I took the plane up to a higher altitude I asked for coordinates to get us to Oahu. All I got was silence. I told my new co-pilot to go back and check on the navigator—see if he was okay. After a minute or so, the co-pilot came back to his seat and said, *Cap, the navigator ain't navigating.*"

"Did he faint or something?' I asked Press.

"I went to find out," Press continued. "I told the co-pilot to take over and I went back to the navigator who was sitting in his seat and looking white as a sheet. I pulled my side arm out of my holster and shoved the barrel of my weapon under his chin," Press gestured as if holding his weapon.

"He must've messed his pants!"

"Probably. I said a few choice words as I demanded to know why he wasn't navigating. The poor kid spit out a few words, but I made him tell me again. I said, *Why the *@#! aren't you navigating? Tell me before I blow your blank-itty-blank head off.* He started crying and he said, *I cheated on my test! I cheated! I don't even know how to navigate.*"

"Oh, no. He lost you all at sea because he didn't know what he was doing?"

"He had no clue. And that's what I told my crew. I used lots of Serbian and English curse words and you don't know how much I wanted to throw that kid out the door. My radar guy said, *Shoot him, Cap!* Only by the grace of God, I didn't. I went back to the cockpit and told the co-pilot that we were on our own. My fuel gauge was reading too low for an aimless trip over the ocean. Talk about a helpless feeling."

"So you were lost at sea. Did you think that was the end?"

"I did. And all those boys were counting on me. I was thinking of their moms and dads and families and how they would receive the horrible news if I didn't find dry land somewhere."

"What happened next?"

"My co-pilot and I looked into the horizon and there was nothing but empty sky and the water line. I kept the plane low to save on fuel and said a lot of silent prayers. After a while we saw a tiny dot in the distance."

"How did you find land in the middle of nowhere?"

"Actually, it wasn't land that I found. It was an American ship."

"What did you do?"

"My crew saw it too and started cheering. I grabbed my lamp and signaled a quick question, *Direction to Hawaiian Islands?* The ship signaled back, *Follow the nose of the ship.* In that instant, at least we had hope. I signaled back, *How far?* The return signal coming back to me said, *Two-hundred miles.*"

"Your crew must have been going nuts."

"Yes they were because they had some hope all of a sudden. I calmed down the cheering and I told the boys that we were running out of fuel and that we still might not make it that far. I ordered everything thrown out. So, the boys threw out everything that wasn't fastened to the plane. A couple of the guys threatened to throw out the navigator. I almost let them."

"Thanks to you, he lived. Right?"

"Yes. The crew threw out all their gear and the ammunition. I shot out the bombsight and they threw it overboard. I didn't want to leave anything for the enemy just in case we didn't make it."

"You were flying blind, I mean as far as knowing were you were. What happened next?"

"I cut back my engines to a lean mix fuel and the plane choked along for miles until we spotted the last island in the Hawaiian chain," Press remarked.

"What were you thinking about that time?"

"Uh, I was thinking about all the bombing runs I had been on and how many times my plane had been hit. I thought about how close I had come to dying by enemy fire. I thought about the napalm runs and how I could have been killed like my best friend, Herbie."

"And suddenly you're about to die because you're running out of fuel."

"Because of some lying kid. I thought about how stupid it would be to die because of that! And I thought about never getting to play professional basketball again. That really made me mad."

If anyone else had said that, it would have been a laugh-line, but Press Maravich was totally serious. He was just as concerned that he may never play ball again.

Press continued, "I radioed the tower and after a few minutes we got a visual of the runway. The plane started sputtering and choking. Like a scene in a movie, I lined it up and inside the plane none of the crew said a word. Firemen and military personnel ran out to the airstrip to witness what would happen. After a few minutes, the wheels of my B-17 touched down. The boys broke out cheering and so did all the personnel at the airstrip. It was quite a sight for everyone. Oh, yeah, I forgot to say ... right when the tires touched the ground, the engines cut off. There wasn't a drop of fuel in the fuel lines when she rolled to stop. Not a drop."

"Sounds like a life-altering experience."

82

"I learned more from a storm, an empty fuel tank, and a lying navigator than I ever learned from Preacher Anderson. That incident got me a lot closer to God."

"And the kid?"

"Did I kill my navigator?" Press laughed. "I'll never tell. No. The poor kid lived and I stayed out of the brig."

Press held in his aging hands a few papers neatly stapled together. On the cover I saw the title: *Two Minutes of Basketball* by Pistol Pete Maravich.

"Okay, enough about me. This should be about Pete," Press stated firmly.

"*Two Minutes of Basketball*," I read the title on the cover sheet aloud.

"I don't want to build a monument to me or Pete. I just want to share what I know with kids all over the world," Press demanded.

"I understand," I replied.

At least, I thought I understood. Press was a humble man whose head was full of years and years of basketball knowledge.

"I used to hold a basketball in my hand and I would use it as an object lesson for my players," Press explained. "I'd tell them, 'This basketball represents all there is to know about basketball, including things that have never been discovered.' Then I would take a magic marker and draw a circle about the circumference of a quarter on the ball. I would say, *See this circle? This circle represents all I have learned in the last fifty years.*"

Press continued to explain that he would then make the tiniest of dots inside the circle. *That little dot is how much of the game you know!*

I got the impression that he must have used that object lesson hundreds of times. That demonstration would have to be in the movie!

"That seemed to always get their attention," Press nodded.

"Press, something tells me you had their attention long before that."

He looked at the typewritten pages carefully and then handed them to me. Press pointed to the cover of the loose pages.

"*Two Minutes of Basketball*," he continued, "I wanted a book that kids could open any time of their day and quickly get some inspiration for their personal game."

"Sounds like a great idea. But did Pete write any of this?" I questioned him gently.

"Let's say he did."

I cocked my head and smiled.

"We'll just say he wrote it. I told you, people will buy it if it says '*Pistol Pete*' on there," Press replied as he stood up and walked to his bedroom.

"But, Press … you wrote it."

"Breakfast in the morning," he continued as he ignored my protest.

"Goodnight, Press."

"Goodnight, Mister Campbell."

The door shut and I retired to the guest bedroom. As I sat on the bed, I whispered a prayer. I thanked God for the precious time I was being given with these amazing American icons. I wondered, *Why me?* I started this project thinking I would write an inspirational movie about a player who changed the game of basketball, but it was obvious there was much more to consider than I had previously envisioned.

Spending time with Press Maravich made me realize that behind most phenomenal talents you'll find a father, a mother, a relative, a teacher or a coach who poured their thoughts and dreams into the next generation.

Pete Maravich had been called the "Elvis Presley" of basketball because he helped change the style and look of how the game was played. Coach Peter "Press" Maravich would be "Pistol Pete's" Colonel Tom Parker. He was the fearless manager and promoter who realized the potential, mapped out a vision, created a plan and then executed that plan.

That night in Clearwater Florida, I realized I was to become not just the screenwriter of a unique American sports story but a biographer and the fortunate author who would chronicle their life story for the world. I would write about what it meant to be the original dreamer as well as the heir to a dream.

CHAPTER 9
Two Minutes of Basketball

When I crawled into bed I was exhausted, but I couldn't stop thinking about where I was and what was happening to me. My intention had been to travel to Florida in order to glean information from Pete's dad so I might get a better handle on who the Maravich men were; more importantly, what made Pete the great player he became. I had confirmed my belief that with any story, there is mostly likely an interesting backstory. It helps the reader or viewer of a film to better understand the character if they know the character's worldview and their upbringing.

During my time as an actor on the soap opera *Another Life* much of my off-screen time was spent in the green room, memorizing lines and discussing all facets of performing arts with the cast. Matt Williams reminded me of important things such as starting my research with character analysis and determining his or her worldview.

As I researched Pete's background, I always kept in mind Matt's words that we are the sum total of our choices in life, but we are also a product of the choices made for us. Especially as children, we have forced upon us the wishes and dreams of our parents. Some might argue that as parents we tend to push too hard to see our dreams fulfilled in our kids. In Pete's life that could be argued to be the case, as he would often mention, *Dad turned me into a basketball robot—an android.* As I lay there, dreaming about the doors opening for me, I understood that there was no doubt that Press, the genius coach in the other room, had helped to mold and shape his son into a basketball superstar.

But there was so much more to discover. Hundreds of dads have worked with their young boys and girls to push, encourage and instruct them to be basketball players. Some have become great basketball players. But there are some boys and girls who only had themselves and maybe an encouraging teacher, relative, pastor or friend to speak some dreams into their imaginations.

In Pete's case his father pushed all the right buttons. Fortunately for the sport of basketball, Pete bought in. Big time. There was no way that Press could have foreseen that his soon would grow to be 6'5" and become the tallest guard in the NBA when he signed with the Atlanta Hawks. But even if he had stopped growing at 5'9" Pete Maravich would have still been a sight to see.

I reached for the chain on the lamp next to the bed, but before I could turn off the light and shut off my brain, I noticed the few pages of *Two Minutes of Basketball* sitting on the nightstand. I picked them up and started reading.

The following paragraphs are the actual pages of text that Press handed to me. I could certainly tell Coach Maravich wrote the document. I could detect in the words that Press is writing as if he is talking to a young "Pistol Pete," his grandsons, or any young basketball enthusiast learning the game.

The title page reads, *"Two Minutes of Basketball With Pistol Pete Maravich. Three-time college All-American at Louisiana State University, Player of the Year. All-time NCAA High Scorer. NBA 10 Years, 5 Times All-NBA All-Star. Louisiana Hall of Fame."*

The following paragraphs are from the nine pages that Press handed me. As best I can tell, they were written in 1986, and they reflect decades of his teaching young players.

87

The tips to become a better basketball player are all in his words and unedited so you can hear his voice and style. Press attempted to keep it simple although he could have drilled deeper into the many complexities of becoming a great basketball player. Press Maravich's nickname was the "Point-a-Minute Man" because he was a terrific shooter in his own right. There was a reason professional owners came looking for Press in the early days of pro basketball. The following statements are principles Press taught to Pete as a child. They are also things he said to players during his college coaching days and at his Homework Basketball camps.

PAGE 1: SCHOOL'S IN

These columns are written for the young of any age. Specifically, we're talking to the basketball player or prospective player up through the high school senior year. If college players learn anything from these columns we want him to benefit from these articles so that it will have a positive effect to becoming a better student-athlete.

Clip the lessons if you like. We're going to be brief. The time you invest should pay at least as good of dividends as you could expect from 120 seconds invested anywhere else.

As you read about basketball, give yourself a chance to earn rich returns: resolve to make your practice sessions pay.

If you seek a spot on your high school varsity or junior varsity, what are you willing to do to earn it?

Succeeding columns will explore all the honorable avenues of basketball, seeking to draw you into an honest examination of yourself and your reasons for wanting to play.

If these lessons widen your knowledge of basketball terms and deepen you interest in this great American game the author will take his reward therefrom. Perhaps we can make your coach's instructional tasks a shade easier.

We're going to try to talk basketball without sliding into jargon. You can be a great basketball player if you have sufficient self-discipline to persevere, your books to keep up your studies, and your eligibility. You must first be a champion with your academics. Basketball is a year-round game and there are many skills to be mastered. Next: We warm to the game.

PAGE 2: YOU AND BASKETBALL

What's your philosophy? What moves you athletically?

Good legs and a relish for competition; a good head and a generous measure of inherited savvy?

Basketball coaches are expected to believe in their sport and to set the best of examples for their student-athletes. I enjoy the game; I belong to it, and so must the beginner.

Basketball offers the youngster a chance to develop his body and eventually to finance his higher education.

Coaches, players and loyal spectators are the game's salesmen. They help make more fans that recognize the game as healthful and rugged.

How does a good basketball player get his skill? By possessing an intense desire to improve by starting out the right way.

In practice you extend yourself. You stretch your intellect by exercising it. On the court, always give your best by intelligent and constant practice. Develop offensive skills. Be repetitive.

Whether you are big or small, tall or short, slow or fast, there is a place for you on the team, but you must have desire, drive discipline and various skills to overcome any handicap you might possess.

Care about basketball if you play it. Do that and do likewise in your studies. You'll greatly improve your chances to be asked to sign on the line for a college grant-in-aid.

With a Godly attitude, your willingness to learn to pay the price will identify you as a basketball player.

PAGE 3: CLASSROOM COMES FIRST

In my own experience I have found that too many high school athletes wait too long to decide whether they want to attend college.

Today, the high school athlete must acknowledge to himself no later than his freshman year that he is entering adolescence, and begin seriously thinking about his future.

Young men can't participate in sports for glory and neglect classroom work. Classwork is not easy—not a bit.

The National Collegiate Athletic Association in conjunction with the University presidents passed Proposition 48 as of January 1986, enforcing stiffer scholastic requirements. They may even grow tougher.

The athlete who loafs in the classroom likely is cheating himself out of an opportunity to earn a higher education with the help of an athletic scholarship.

He must take the college entrance examination board (Scholastic Aptitude Test) or the ACT, the American College Testing program exam. Leading athletic conferences require one or the other. Moreover, each conference sets up a "cutoff" score. If the athlete falls below the minimum score of 700 he loses his chances of receiving an athletic scholarship.

90

Pursuing a college curriculum is far from easy.

The college student needs mental stamina to keep up. From one to three hours of homework may suffice for the high school athlete. In college he will have to triple his homework and study time.

The athlete must make the most of educational opportunities in high school and college. There are no scholastic short cuts for the athlete.

He can become one of the four kinds of student-athletes: excellent student and equally outstanding athlete; fine athlete and poor student, capable student and poor athlete, or he could stop on the bottom run as both a poor student and poor athlete. The category he stops on depends largely on him.

Know your goal early. Prepare yourself academically now to accept this challenge to be an outstanding student-athlete.

PAGE 4: WE WARM TO THE GAME

"Cool it, man," may be good advice under some circumstances. If you're going to play basketball, however, you'll want to warm to it. Well-tempered enthusiasm and positive attitude belongs on the practice and game courts.

Eventually, you will understand how Pete Rose of the Cincinnati Reds baseball team could say; "I get a thrill every time I put on this Cincinnati uniform." Pete Rose meant it. Other great players of other sports have uttered the same thing.

This writer enjoys basketball, but God comes first without apology. He admires the fine men in it. You needn't apologize for indulging lightly into hero worship of your favorite player.

Your interest will grow as you come to know athletes whose high ideals have been put to the test and have come through the stronger for it.

The post-graduate world looks for and, frankly admires men who can get along with others, who play fair, who play by the rules, who are not ashamed to be industrious, who respect their superiors, who have good health habits, who take victory with humble pride and take defeat with grace. The men and women can win through adversity.

Warm to the game. Go further—enjoy basketball! Your "cool" friend may not understand at first. If they don't come around—never mind. It is better to be unappreciated by some than to miss the fun you can find in basketball.

As you play the game better, give ear to Oliver Wendell Holmes: "The world wants leaders, thinkers, doers—men of power and action; men who can step out from the crowd and lead instead of follow." Cool it, indeed!

Give the game everything you have. Become one of Mr. Holmes' "leader-thinker-doers."

PAGE 5: THE ART OF SHOOTING - PART 1

The thrill of the game is in the shooting. The object of the game is to "put the ball through the hoop." "Pistol Pete," college basketball's greatest scorer, practiced thousands of hours of shooting.

This is what attracts the youngster who enjoys shooting the most. Anyone can become a good shooter if he will dedicate time to practice.

Start by learning the basic stance adequate for most shots.

Let's begin with the feet and work up. Set your feet as if you were standing at attention. Then, spread your feet six-to-eight inches and advance the right foot about five inches. Your knees should be bent about five degrees forward and your shoulders rounded a little and squared toward the basket.

You are ready for the ball. Grip it in both hands as if to make a test pass. Hands are on the sides of the ball—fingers spread slightly, palms free and not touching the ball. The thumbs point 45 degrees toward the goal. Make certain you could draw a horizontal line between the thumbs—spread about two inches. Now, slide your left hand upward toward the top of the ball. This little adjustment keeps the same spread of two inches, but now there is a 45-degree angle between the left and right thumb. Lift the ball so that you are looking at its bottom. Notice the big picture window between your forearms; the result of the previous adjustment.

Hold the ball where there is a straight line, but angled about 10 to 15 degrees from your nose to your right thumb or left thumb if you are a southpaw ... and eight inches out front.

You must now imagine. Create an image in the back of your mind of the big picture of you doing the shooting.

You are now ready to try the first shot. Start close to the basket on the right side and about five feet out. This shot is popular because of the higher percentage of returns.

PAGE 6: THE ART OF SHOOTING - PART 2

The previous lesson dealt with the basic stance. I believe that youngsters 6 to 8 years old should not start shooting with the regulation size ball.

They should have a biddy-type—smaller than the regular ball. There are many brands on the market.

The basket should not be more than seven or eight feet high to guard against developing bad shooting habits ... which might be difficult to correct.

An 8-year-old should aim and shoot the ball one foot above his age; nine feet should be the limit of his shooting area around the basket. As he ages and gets stronger he will increase the distance. This enables the novice to become a high percentage shooter.

Remember these hints to become a high-percentage shooter.

1. Holding the ball: Don't forget finger pad control, palms free of ball, grip nice and firm—left hand higher than the right.

2. Keep your elbow straight when you follow through. Snap your wrist and put backspin on the ball.

3. Shoot to score. In your mind, see the ball going through the hoop. If you miss, then "hang" the ball on the rim for possible tip-ins by the bigger players.

4. If you are close to the basket, use the glass boards for 45-degree shots to increase our percentage.

5. If you have a favorite shot, practice that more than the others ... but keep adding to your repertoire.

6. Learn to shoot with either hand.

7. If you aren't using the backboard, then on all other shots use the front and side of the rim.

8. Practice releasing the ball quickly.

9. See the goal (hoop) with both eyes. Don't be a one-eyed shooter or your depth perception will be poor.

10. Make certain your trajectory is high enough.

11. Find the time—better yet—make the time for yourself to practice a lot.

12. Have confidence in your ability to shoot and be patient when you are learning.

13. Don't shot put or throw the ball—shoot it!

14. Get the big picture—project a good image of shooting. Don't worry about missed shots. Work on form. Try to analyze WHY you're missing; keep plugging and don't lose your concentration. The youngster who budgets extra time for his shooting will succeed.

Do the small things well and acquire confidence and courage. As a beginner, you lack polish, but you can become a skilled shooter with time and patience. Once you possess the correct form, your results will rapidly improve. Be repetitive in shooting. Do not get discouraged, but continue doing the same things and our shot will get better.

After reading the pages Press had given me, I was struck by the pure love for the sport that Press possessed. But I was impressed by much more than that. Basketball wasn't just a passion or something he loved, it was a lifestyle that Press embraced and passed on to his children. It was platform for him to dispense knowledge and offer practical information that a young person could use in order to build his or her character.

I remember hoping I would get the chance to spend time with Press again. The time I did get with him had profoundly affected my thinking about the man.

At this stage in Press Maravich's life he was part coach and part wise old fatherly sage. He possessed a wealth of knowledge and in many ways he embodied the American Dream. Pete considered Press to be a brilliant basketball mentor. The father and son duo had become two adult gentlemen who had forged a solid friendship through the fires of adversity.

I pondered the longevity of their closeness and what bound them. Press and Pete were united by the same blood, vision and dreams. After nearly four decades together they were still sharing the same quest of impacting a sport to which they had already given so much.

CHAPTER 10
Bigger Than Us

Clearwater will always hold a wonderful place in my memory because of my few days spent there with Pete and Press. I had been to Florida on business and personal appearances as an actor, but in many ways I felt as if I were visiting that beautiful state for the first time. Riding in the car with Pete and Press, eating at their favorite places and spending time in their vacation homes made me feel as though I was in the middle of a family reunion, not conducting book interviews.

Pete drove us to the airport, and I am eternally grateful that he never stopped filling my head, my recorder and my notepad with useful information. As Pete described in full color his unique childhood exploits, they played out in my mind like the movie we wanted to create.

"When I was a kid, I would sneak out my bedroom window at night and play basketball in the driveway," Pete began. "Many times I climbed out during a rain storm. I didn't care if it was lightning or windy, or whatever; I would go out and dribble and shoot in the rain."

"Did you get in trouble with your parents?" I wondered.

"Mom would say something about it—but Dad? Are you kidding? He probably wished he had thought it up first. See, my dad was an originator. He was the inventor and innovator of all the crazy drills because he wanted to challenge me to be the best."

"How old were you when he started giving you drills to do?"

"I was really young. I just remember he would wake up in the morning and jot down new drills to test out on me. You got to understand that ninety percent of my conversations with Pop were about basketball. If I hadn't sneaked out my window the first time during that rain storm, I bet you he would have come up with that drill at some point."

"I'm trying to picture this," I stopped him. "In fact, it would make a good scene in the movie; a little kid out in the driveway dribbling in a rain storm."

"At night, with lightning," Pete added.

"We can do that. Frank has probably directed that scene in his head already!"

I could tell that Pete was warming to the idea of his story being a Hollywood movie. He started telling childhood stories as if he was directing a film.

"People misunderstood my dad sometimes. People who liked him, really liked him, but people who wrote about us … like in newspapers and magazines … they weren't too sure."

"What do you mean? They thought he was too hard on you?"

"Or, they couldn't wrap their minds around the father and son, coach and player relationship. I lived with the coach. I got attention from my coach twenty-four seven. There was never a break from basketball. But you've got to remember, it wasn't just my father pushing me. It was me pushing me. Pop always talked about the three D's: desire, discipline and dedication. That's what we teach in my 'Pistol Pete' Camps in the summer. I can tell kids all about fundamentals and the right way to dribble, shoot and pass, but if they don't have the three D's, they'll never be exceptional players."

"Break it down for me … the three D's."

98

"Discipline is a kid practicing his skills every single day; over and over and over. Darrel, I would shoot a thousand shots a day if I could. You shoot when your body aches. You shoot when you're tired. Discipline makes you do it."

I recalled our being in the gym in California a few weeks before this trip. As I watched Pete shoot, I wondered how many thousands of shots Pete's wrist had flicked toward an iron hoop during his life. I had never known a professional basketball player, especially one who derived a paycheck because he could play a game to the highest level.

There was a reason that nearly every shot that Pete performed found its mark. He simply had done it so many times correctly that the results came easily.

"Dedication is like a marriage," Pete continued. "You pledge yourself to the sport. You're not going to leave it or work on another sport. You marry basketball and dedicate yourself to it. That sounds strange, but that's what it is. And then, there is desire. One problem, though … desire can't be taught. It can be encouraged, but a kid either has desire or he doesn't. Kinda like trying to teaching a kid to be taller," Pete laughed at his remark.

"Hey, I had a short mom and dad!" I replied, defending shorter people everywhere. "I remember a kid on my little league team like that. He wanted the uniform and he wanted to be on our team but he had no desire to get better, so my dad couldn't put him on the field. Funny thing was, the kid didn't care. His mother was always really upset that he didn't get to play, but the kid wasn't. You're right. You can't teach desire."

"When I was a kid," Pete continued, "my main desire besides playing basketball was to make money by playing pool and pinball."

"You actually made money?"

99

"Back in the early 1960s, they had pinball machines that spit out money if you won the game. When Pops was the coach at Clemson I spent a lot of time in a pool hall downtown betting people, playing pool and winning a nickel at a time playing pinball. If I wasn't somewhere shooting a basketball, I was in the pool hall betting on games."

"Were you good at it?" I asked.

"You know it. I won a lot, and that's how I had money for soda pop and burgers back then. I remember one day a government guy came in the place to see if people were betting. Like everywhere but Las Vegas, betting was illegal."

Pete painted the story as if he were pitching me the movie version.

"We stopped gambling when the government guy walked in wearing his fancy suit and tie. During one of his surprise visits he pulled a pool cue out of the wall rack and put chalk on the tip as he looked around the room and asked, *You wanna play me?* I told him I'd play him. I racked the balls and he broke. In just a few minutes he ran the table as the other guys and I looked on. After the last ball fell in the pocket, he hung the cue stick back in the rack and he lit a cigarette like Paul Newman in *The Hustler*. He said, '*Don't you boys be gambling, ya hear?*'"

"Should we put that in the movie?" I asked.

"You could. He was a mysterious guy. I don't know what division of the government he was from, but I know he was making sure there was no gambling going on."

"What about the pinball?"

"Like I said, I played pinball games, too. Back in those days you could win money playing pinball machines. You were supposed to be eighteen years old to play, but I played anyway when the government guy wasn't around."

"What was your secret to winning?" I asked.

"Those old machines were different. You could rock them and they wouldn't tilt and stop on you. One time, I won six hundred games and the payoff was thirty dollars!" Pete laughed.

I could picture the young Pete Maravich demanding that the machine bend to his will.

"I had a college freshman go up and collect the money for me because I was still too young to be playing for money," Pete continued. "I loaded up on Cokes and Moon Pies and snacks. That's how I made money instead of mowing yards and raking leaves like the other kids."

"Did your dad ever give you an allowance?"

"Heck, no. He wasn't making much money. He made ninety-six dollars a week at Clemson, I think. One day I saw a pellet gun in a store window and I imagined going out and shooting a bird or something with it. In my little kid imagination, I thought it might have enough power to blow down a wall. You know how we are as little kids. You just wanna kill something or knock something down for some reason," Pete laughed at the thought.

"So you begged your dad for the gun?"

"On Saturday morning my dad and the assistant coach at Clemson University went down to that store with me to buy the gun but when we got there I put my hands in my pockets and I realized I'd forgotten my money. Oh, Dad was really mad."

"Did he loan you money for the gun?"

"No! No way. You would've thought it was the end of the world when I told him I forgot my money. He stood there with the coach and waited while I ran all the way back home to get my money."

101

"You sound like you had a pretty normal childhood off the basketball court. Did you have a girlfriend at that age?"

"Not really. I was just starting to understand how different and how cute girls were but I didn't have any desire for a girlfriend. There was a girl who lived next door who was really cute and getting older, I'll say."

We laughed at Pete's attempt to describe a young girl who was blossoming into a young lady.

"You know what I mean. Well, she would have her light on in her bedroom at night and I guess she didn't mind someone looking in on her when she was changing her clothes and getting ready for bed."

Pete tilted his head to me, making sure I understood where he was going with the story.

"My friend and I sneaked over and climbed into a really big shrub that grew under her bedroom window. We were holding real still and not making a sound as we peeked in her window. Well, all of a sudden, a bird landed in the shrub just above my friend and that stupid bird pooped on my friend's head."

"No way!" I laughed.

"It really happened! I started laughing and that got the attention of the girl's dogs. The dogs started barking at us and a few minutes later the pretty girl's dad burst out the back door with a shotgun! We ran through the dark as fast as we could."

"Did that girl find out you were hiding outside her window?"

"I don't think so," Pete laughed.

"I'm not sure we'll shoot that scene. I'm hoping for a G-rating," I joked.

"Hey, you could write a scene about the first girl I had a crush on."

"Your wife?"

"I'm talking about when I was a kid. I got my first kiss at a birthday party. I remember it was the first time I got interested in something other than basketball. I was standing on her front porch and she grabbed my face and kissed me."

"Now, there's a good movie moment," I commented.

"It was incredible to me as a kid. I didn't know what to do. I mean, I didn't know anything about girls or what to do with them if I had feelings for them."

"You were normal."

"Eleven or twelve years old. All I remember is when she kissed me it was like I went deaf. I couldn't hear anything. I just stared at her and she stared back and that was that," Pete explained, and then he waited for a beat. "I guess you had to be there."

We laughed as Pete pulled up to the curb in front of the airport to let us out.

"You guys have a good trip. When do you want to get back together?" Pete asked.

"What's your schedule look like?" I wondered.

"I'm going to be in Los Angeles with Meadowlark Lemon—publicity pictures and interviews. We'll get together and go see a Laker game. I'll arrange things with Frank."

"You know where to find me," I replied. "Thanks for everything. I'll be praying for your dad."

"Thanks, Darrel."

"Thank you. Let's keep this going," I told him.

We shook hands and our Florida visit ended. Our objectives had become clearer. Frank would pursue a deal with book publishers because after hearing all the stories we were both completely convinced that our efforts would include turning Pete's life story into a book before we made a movie.

The low budget independent feature we had planned to make would not be big enough to hold all of the stories of these legends. The wheels were turning and Frank, the guy who had introduced me to this venture, had marketing and promotion ideas swirling in his head.

"We'll hold auditions in Louisiana," Frank said. "The kid has to be from Louisiana. The investors will like that and support that."

Frank assured me that he would immediately contact his alma mater Louisiana State University. He was focused on bringing attention to LSU as well as the film so it was his goal to hold the movie auditions there. He envisioned making the "Pistol Pete" movie auditions a media event. He launched into telling me all about the TV and newspaper people he knew personally that he could invite to the auditions. And he wanted at least one side of the arena full of kids and their parents.

I worked as a professional actor in New York and Los Angeles, and Frank's description of *The Pistol* movie audition wasn't anything like what I had experienced. Usually, an actor studies his or her audition script or perfects a monologue and then stands and performs before casting directors whose decision can change the course of one's life forever. It's the worst type of job interview, in my opinion. Now that I'm a director sitting on the other side of the table, my heart goes out to performers who read for my projects. I see the trembling hands and I want to tell them, *I've been there and you'll be okay!*

Frank saw the opportunity as a good public relations moment and a situation where Pete could meet all the hopefuls and sign autographs. But first he wanted to call some publishers and get the book negotiations rolling. Suddenly, what began as a notion to write a screenplay and produce it, turned into an effort to help Pete create multiple products.

CHAPTER 11
Pete, Press, Helen Montini

Neatly placed in my briefcase, I had a handful of micro-cassettes with my sports idol's voice on them. Pete and Press telling personal stories of their past would always be a treasure to me regardless of whether the book was ever published or not. I opened my small spiral notebook on which I made my notes, and now the words had more meaning to me. They weren't just words on a page but the tone and rhythm of Press and Pete's voices on tape.

What a privilege it was to have been in their presence and to have witnessed their emotions. Friendships were developing and I had met my hero's father—my hero's hero.

I closed my eyes and remembered Press sitting in his chair at his condominium. He was so kind to me and so open about who he was. He was also candid about what he wished the world to know about his son, Pete. I'll never forget how intent and focused he was that night as he rattled off story after story that made up their eventful lives.

The unsettling news that Press had bone cancer had ramped up the urgency for me to gather as much information as possible. Fortunately for me, Press wanted to get his personal history off his chest so I could communicate to readers just how passionate he was about Pete.

No one was a more enthusiastic fan of Pistol Pete Maravich than Press Maravich. But Press was the original dreamer in the family who had used basketball to help him flee poverty and the confines of working in a steel mill.

Press was the original Maravich goal-setter who had a keen understanding that basketball could be more than a sport. It could be a way of life, a career and a stage for entertainment. Press considered basketball a vehicle for change.

I looked at my notes again and smiled as I realized the trip to Clearwater had many surprises. For one, I had never thought of Pistol Pete Maravich as a communicator or storyteller, but he was definitely both.

My exposure to hearing Pete speak or observing him during interviews was terribly limited. When "Pistol Pete" was playing basketball there were only three TV channels broadcast into my small town. Well, there may have been four channels, if you count the fuzzy UHF channel that was hard to view. I can't recall hearing Pete speak much at all back in those days other than perhaps a line on an occasional TV commercial.

Fans of Pete read about him in *Sports Illustrated* or we caught a highlight now and then, so his "voice," had to somehow come through his quotes in the print media. However, I soon learned that his teammates and a few persons he befriended in college or during his professional career knew well that Pete was smart, witty and extremely talkative if in the right mood.

Before I spent time with Pete and Press, I considered them to be men who possessed a wealth of basketball knowledge and skills. My opinion of Press was that he was a hard-driving coach who handed down to his spectacularly gifted son the dream of being the greatest basketball player in the world. As I look back and remember my time with both Maravich legends, I think fondly of their abilities as artful communicators, deftly spinning yarns and communicating stories full of surprising detail, color and humor.

106

As the plane lifted off for the long flight back to Los Angeles I closed my eyes and I could hear Press's voice as he told me his stories.

"You boys been hopping freight trains?" one of the Pittsburg Pirates asked a young Press Maravich.

"We sure did, Mister," Press told the player with pride. "My buddies and I hopped trains to New Castle and our next adventure, we're gonna jump on a train to Cleveland."

"You boys must really love baseball."

"Yah, but this time we're not going to see baseball. We're going to the air races!" Press explained.

The thought of watching acrobatic planes competing was where Press first got the notion to become a pilot. The Pittsburgh Pirate player, whose name Press couldn't recall, looked at Press and his friends with an eye to their futures. Each of the young guys had a juicy wad of chewing tobacco tucked in their cheek, trying to emulate what they thought it meant to look like a professional ball player. The Pirate, showing some concern for the boys, took a moment to speak wisdom into their lives.

"Boys, I wouldn't be hopping trains if I were you," the player warned.

"Why not?" Press asked.

"You can't play ball if one of those things cuts you in half," he cautioned with a fatherly tone.

Leaving Press and the boys with that thought, the player turned around and zipped the baseball from the center field fence, bouncing it into home plate. It was clear that he was showing off the power of his arm to the tobacco-chewing youngsters.

Press heard the words of caution, but what the Pirate player didn't realize was that the power of Press's thoughts and imagination were being spurred on by the player's dire warning. Press was strong-willed, determined, and dead-set on getting out of Aliquippa, Pennsylvania to take on the world. It would take more than words of caution and fear to hold him back from his dream.

I slid my headphones into place as the plane reached its cruising altitude. I carefully inserted tape #1 into the recorder. I was thrilled that I possessed more than written notes and memories, but I was blessed to capture their unique voices. *If this is what being an author feels like I think I could get used to it,* I thought to myself.

"I used the same determination I had as a kid, I guess," the familiar voice of Press flowed through my headphones. "Suddenly, I was older and somehow I had survived a World War. Not to mention, I was the only one of my brothers and sisters who survived the influenza outbreak. I was just stubborn and bull-headed enough not to get myself killed, I guess.

Although death had taken most of Press Maravich's family and many of his friends, he refused to turn bitter towards life. He used the tragedy to motivate himself to wring every last drop out of the life he had been given. Instead of staying where he had been planted in the beginning of his life, Press broke the family mold and forged a fresh new path of his own despite the odds against him.

To Press, serving during WWII was just a terrible distraction from what he knew he could be. Watching that Pittsburg Pirate throw the ball to home plate was a tangible metaphor for his childhood dreams. He was determined to lean back and use all his strength to hit the target of his ultimate vision of playing basketball on a professional level.

108

I listened carefully to the gruff sounding voice. Now, when I say "gruff," I don't mean ill tempered or harsh. His voice was just strong and weathered from decades of use. After years of shouting at his players the strain had taken a toll on his voice box. Just think of the millions of words of instruction, encouragement and frustration uttered during his fifty years of coaching!

"All I could think about was basketball," Press continued. "I got home from the Pacific and in my mind I kept thinking of playing and coaching at the Anacostia Naval Air Station, the Hawaiian Islands Championship, and the random tournaments with my fellow sailors and airmen in the South Pacific. I couldn't get out of my head the championship with the Eagles, and I never wanted to forget those memories."

There was a man named Paul Birch who heard that Press was coming to the end of his duties as a Naval officer. At the time, Press was serving as a flight instructor in Pensacola, Florida.

"I got a letter from Coach Birch. He was coaching the Youngstown Bears professional basketball team and he had tracked me down. Believe it or not, I had to make a decision whether I was going to go teach the Chinese how to fly airplanes over and around the Himalayan Mountains or take the offer from the Bears to play basketball. Before too long I traded my Navy uniform for a Youngstown Bears uniform and I was back in professional basketball."

I could tell by the tone in his voice that those must have been bittersweet memories. He had given up one passion for another.

"Remember, that's what my future wife was going to ask of me anyway," Press reminded. "Helen wanted my feet on the ground and she wanted me to coach for a living."

After thirty games or so with the Bears, Chick Davies of the Pittsburgh Iron Men gave Press a call, and by 1946 Press was firmly in place as a star with the team. His dream of working hard and living life as a professional basketball player had been met with success and he was content.

Looking at the pictures Pete had shown me of his dad during his pro years as a Youngstown Bear gave me a better idea of Press's public personae. The person I had spent time with in Clearwater—the man who had just received devastating news that he had bone cancer—was a strong, but a gentle soul. He was a man now in his sunset years who was taking an account of the spectacular and colorful life that he and his son had experienced together. His words had an edge of eagerness and yet a tone of finality to them.

"Pistol Pete's" dad didn't just pass down his knowledge of the game of basketball and the game of life to his impressionable young son; he passed down a fiery passion that he held deep within his soul. Life was not just to be lived; it was to be experienced with zeal and danger and a sense of accomplishment. Taking chances on freight trains and fighter-bombers was just part of the deal with Press, which brings me to the story of how Press met Pete's mother, Helen.

"My name is Press Maravich," Press remarked to the alluring young woman behind the taxi dispatch desk.

Pictures of the dashing young Press Maravich gave me some hint to the charm of the man. Had Press possessed any aspirations to be on the big screen, I believe he could have taken his chiseled jaw line and intense eyes into any casting office in Hollywood and landed a role. The battle-hardened Navy officer and professional basketball player was about to meet the first person in his life who could buckle and weaken his knees.

110

"What's with all the stitches?" the dark-haired beauty asked Press.

For a moment, Press had forgotten he had been sewn up like the seam of a football after his last game. I think of basketball as being a tough sport today, but in the 1940s it was common for the players to take all kinds of cheap shots to the face that would often require medical attention.

"They called the Iron Men the 'Iron Five' for a reason," Press laughed.

Those guys were men's men who battled for the minutes they played—five warriors who threw elbows, punches and jabs to the ribs as they earned a few bucks playing basketball.

As Press admired the hatcheck girl, he disregarded how the stitches over one of his eyes and sutures near his mouth made him look. He smiled carefully and turned on his charm.

"Are you a boxer?"

"No, I'm a professional basketball player."

"Basketball, huh?"

"That's right. The greatest sport in America and the most exciting sport ever. Press Maravich. Pittsburgh Ironman," Press introduced himself and then waited for the young lady to respond with her introduction.

With the same boldness that Press displayed, she introduced herself. "Helen Gravor," she announced.

"Nice name," Press winked.

"You should come to a game sometime and see what it's all about," Press encouraged her. "There's lots of excitement and you could see what I do."

Helen appreciated the boldness of the dashing young man as he leaned on the dispatch desk. She laughed at his brashness, but inside, his demeanor immediately impressed her.

"Whaddya say you and I go to dinner sometime? Press asked with confidence as he assumed a positive response.

Helen coyly avoided any quick response to the fascinating stranger. She pretended to work as her eyes scanned the room to detect anyone who might be watching. After a few awkward moments, Helen finally replied.

"When?"

"Do you work on Friday nights?" Press asked, trying to corral an answer.

"As a matter of fact, I'm off that night," Helen replied with a nervous twist of her hair.

Press quickly acquired Helen's number and he made arrangements regarding their date for Friday night. Unfortunately, at the last minute, the basketball team was called out of town. On Friday Press found himself playing basketball miles away from Pittsburgh and he had been unable to contact Helen to cancel their first date.

Meanwhile, Helen sat at home, waiting for her charming prince to show up at her door. Her hair was carefully styled and she was impeccably dressed. Helen was nervous and excited for a dinner date with the handsome professional athlete. Unfortunately, Press never showed.

A few days passed and Press and his team returned to town. Shortly after checking back into the hotel, Press mustered his courage and sauntered back to the dispatch desk in the hotel and threw himself on the mercy of Helen Gravor. He feared it might not turn out well, but he had to make amends. There was something special about Helen.

112

Press endured several minutes of hearing Helen's story about how long she had waited and how much she felt like an idiot for trusting some strange, arrogant guy with stitches in his head. It was time for Press to beg.

"It was stupid! I am stupid. I should've tried harder to get word to you that we were going out of town. I'm so dumb, Helen. Please, please, forgive me. It will never, ever happen again. I promise. You don't know me, but I don't break promises. Please, forgive me, Helen. Please, I'm beggin' ya! Please."

Press told me that he could've made an even bigger scene in the hotel lobby but Helen extended grace to her charming suitor and she forgave him on the spot.

"I forgive you."

"Thank you! How about this Saturday night? Please, say you'll give me a second chance," Press pleaded.

Press and Helen were destined to be together. I had heard stories about a man and woman pledging their undying love to each other on a first date but I had never met anyone who actually did it. At Bill Green's Nightclub in Pittsburgh, the big band performed popular tunes like "Chattanooga Choo Choo" as Press and Helen sat at their candlelit table enjoying a wonderful meal. Press was dressed in a dark suit and tie and Helen wore a black dress. The atmosphere was full of joy and hope. The war was over and Press and Helen were happy, employed and single. For an hour they enjoyed delicious food, laughed and shared stories about themselves.

"By the time I asked Helen to dance our first dance, I felt as if I had known her for years. Oh, she was so lovely and she smelled like flowers. Her face was kind and she had an innocence about her that made me want to take care of her," Press explained.

The band began playing a slow love song, which was Press's motivation to get Helen on the dance floor. He desired to have Helen in his arms. Press could feel his heart beating as he longed for her.

"I looked into her dark eyes and I couldn't believe what I was thinking. My mind kept saying, *Ask her to marry you, you idiot!* When you know, you know," Press recollected.

Press led Helen across the dance floor and she danced gracefully.

"It was as if we were in a movie," Press said. "I kept looking into her eyes and wondering why this miracle was happening to me. Suddenly I just blurted, "We should be married.""

Helen missed a step or two in the dance as the statement took her aback.

"Married?" Helen asked.

"Married," Press continued with his trademark boldness. "You and me ... we should be married."

Helen could tell that Press was as serious as she had ever seen him during their brief acquaintance.

"Let's sit for a minute," Press urged.

Helen took Press by the hand and they walked back to the table. Helen's attitude toward her new suitor unexpectedly shifted to serious and somber. Press observed her body language as she folded her hands and avoided any eye contact.

"What's wrong?" Press asked. He was beginning to mentally kick himself, afraid his suggestion of marriage had just ruined the special night.

"I don't think you would want to marry someone like me," Helen replied as her eyes darted around the room.

"Why not?" Press asked.

Press was surprised by her remark and had to have an answer. Something had gone terribly wrong and he couldn't imagine what was coming next. He was gazing at the most attractive woman he had ever met. She was kind. She had a beauty on the inside that he could feel.

"I couldn't understand why she had suddenly turned," Press said.

Being with Helen that night was like nothing he had ever experienced. All he felt was admiration and love bubbling up inside him.

"I was afraid that she simply wasn't feeling what I was feeling," Press said.

"Helen Montini is my real name; my married name," she continued without emotion.

Her declaration hit Press like cold water.

"Your married name?"

She nodded.

"You're married? What is this?"

Anger swelled inside Press. He was a man of character and suddenly he was feeling hoodwinked. He slammed back the remainder of his drink and he was ready to storm out of the room when Helen stopped him.

"Wait! Wait, Press. It's not what you think. I was married," Helen added cautiously, not wanting to add any more harm to the moment.

Helen couldn't force herself to make eye contact with Press. What she had to tell him next could send everything into the opposite direction depending solely upon his reaction.

Typically, Press drove conversations. Up to this moment in their young relationship he had dominated the talking. Suddenly, he found himself sitting silently as he waited for Helen to continue at her own pace.

"I was married to someone I loved very much. My husband was in the military, like you were. I couldn't imagine my life with any other man."

Her words stabbed at Press's heart.

"But my husband was killed in Europe during the war."

"My heart sank when Helen revealed that news to me," Press continued. "I remembered my friend Herbie who had hugged his loved ones goodbye hoping to return to their arms someday. I always felt guilty for making it back alive when so many true heroes didn't."

Press was taken aback by the revelation and not sure how to respond. He felt compassion for Helen. All Press could muster was, "I'm so sorry. I can't imagine what you have been through."

Helen wiped a tear from her face as Press fished for some way to smooth the somber moment.

"I could never replace him. I know that," Press assured her.

"But, there's one more thing," Helen continued with a crack in her voice.

There was more to come. It was obvious that Helen had been gravely wounded by life, and the precious soul sitting across from him was ready to be vulnerable and open to a virtual stranger. *What could be next?* Press wondered to himself. *Was there more sorrow and tragedy? Was there another reason why they couldn't or shouldn't be together?*

Press began to regret that he had been so bold about asking her to marry him. He felt he should have taken things much slower. As he looked into her tear-filled eyes, he ached for her. Press began to see her as a damaged flower. The confidence she had shown before was wilting.

116

Helen was beautiful, but not whole. Suddenly, Press was consumed with compassion, and he wanted even more to let her know that she was safe with him.

"What is it, Helen? You can tell me. What else?"

"I have a child."

Press pretended to not be shocked.

"Okay."

"A little boy," Helen continued.

At this stage in Press's life it was difficult to catch him off guard. But as Press told me the heartfelt story, he made it clear that Helen was keeping him off balance.

"A boy, huh? Hmmm. That's ... something," Press nodded as he tried to stay engaged and interested.

Helen was afraid that this piece of personal information would be a deal breaker regarding any future relationship. There were plenty of young and available single ladies who had been waiting years for American men to return from WWII. Most of them probably didn't have the heartache and burden of a young child attached to their lives. Helen expected Press to graciously bow out of the situation and tell her "goodnight."

"A three-year-old. He is what I have left of my former life," Helen added and waited nervously for Press's response.

"Three. Poor little tyke," Press replied.

Press was battle-tested and sure of who he was as a man. He possessed the heart of a lion and at times a heart that was softened by realities of life and death. Like many young, single men, the first thought of actually being a father and raising a child was a bit breathtaking. However, just the thought of Helen's toddler growing up without a dad as Press had been forced to do, was more than Press could bear.

"I never knew my father."

117

"Really?" Helen asked.

"I was raised by a stepdad. My father was killed in a work accident. I don't have any memory of him," Press replied.

"Not at all?" Helen asked.

"Nothing. I would've given anything to have a Dad in my life."

Press took Helen's hand, and he tried to comfort her as he gazed into her worried eyes. There was no question in his mind about wanting to be with Helen forever. God had brought the two of them together in an unlikely place and during a time so full of questions. Since childhood, Press had been hopping freight trains and traveling wherever life would take him. Taking chances was his way of life.

Press broke the silence again as he asked, "Helen Montini, I know this sounds crazy, but I love you. I love everything about you. I will love everything I will learn about you. Will you be my wife? Will you become Helen Maravich?"

Helen sat silent. Press expected an immediate reply, even if it were "no." Surely all the surprises the beautiful widow and single mother had to deliver had been exhausted. Helen had successfully jumped over two of the three hurdles. Press wasn't shaken that Helen had been married and he wasn't thrown off balance by the announcement of her being a mother and widow.

"You're a widow with a baby boy. Is that it?" He implored.

"There is one more thing," Helen started again cautiously. "Press, I know it must seem like I'm trying to run you off, but marriage is forever as far as I'm concerned."

118

"Of course. I feel the same way. What is it? What else could there be?"

"You said you'd like to get a job as an airline pilot?"

"That's right. If I'm going to be a husband and a dad, I can't be running around the country playing basketball. I need a more stable job that will keep me around you and my new son more often, and I'll need a job that will pay the bills," Press replied with the assurance of a responsible husband-to-be. "You would be the proud wife of a professional airline pilot."

"I don't want you to be a pilot," Helen announced.

"You don't? Why?"

Helen stiffened and with a worried look she was playing out in her mind the reality of her husband flying around the country and being far from home. It only brought a fear of loss to her mind. The thought of another husband being killed and taken suddenly from her and her boy was more than she could bear.

Press tried to explain to her that being a pilot was the profession in which he had the most experience and something in which he truly excelled.

"I'm sure you're a fine pilot," she complimented.

"I am the best."

His confident reply gave Helen the impression that the notion of their being married was quickly fading.

"I guess this wasn't such a good idea," Helen replied, as she feared the night would come to an abrupt conclusion.

"Hold on," Press stopped her, "Just ... hold on a minute."

"I'm being selfish, I know, but I'm thinking of my little boy as well. He's already lost a father," Helen said.

119

Press was already envisioning their wedding. His friends would be so jealous if Press walked into a room with Helen on his arm. And he would be so proud to call her his wife. But, there was more than beauty attracting him to her. Helen's voice was sweet and tender and her smile captivated him. In his imagination, they were the perfect couple destined to be together.

"It's kind of crazy," she squirmed.

"I know."

"I'm asking too much of you," she admitted, "Press, I understand if you want to just walk away, but think about this; all of the stories you've told me seem to have basketball connected to them," Helen continued with one more attempt to sway him.

All the while the little voice in his head was screaming, "Don't let her go!"

"I can't play basketball forever," Press chimed in.

It was the break that Helen was looking for.

"No, but you can be a coach until you retire!"

Press hadn't given that option much thought. He was still a player and coaching would be something he could consider doing in the future.

"A coach," Press pondered.

"Yes!" Helen brightened. "You could be one of the best coaches this country has ever known. You're smart and you've played the game at the highest level. It's obviously a passion of yours. You do love it, right?"

"More than anything, really," Press nodded. "It's not flying, but I've never really given much thought about coaching as a job."

"For me? Would you do it for me?"

My heart ached for Press who had been a widower for many years at the time of our interview. He had wanted to be a pilot, and he had set a course toward that noble profession. The decision he made that night for Helen Montini was the decision that set in motion the rest of his life's work. It also set the stage for the legend of Peter "Press" Maravich and his future son Pistol Pete Maravich.

Press continued to tell me of his dreams and how so many of them had come true. He longed to leave the steel mills, and he did. He wanted to serve his country, and he became a decorated WW II bomber pilot. He wished to become a professional athlete, and he played basketball with the World Champion Detroit Eagles, the Youngstown Bears and his favorite team, the Pittsburgh Iron Men. He dreamed of being one of the best players in the nation, and he became one of the top scoring guards in the professional leagues. He wanted to compete against the best, and he played against historic figures such as Dutch Denhert, Nat Holman and many others. But sitting in front of him that night in Pittsburgh was his ultimate dream. He wanted to find the perfect woman to marry.

"For you, Helen, I'll become a coach. In fact, I'll become anything you want me to be," Press assured her.

They stood up by their table and gave each other a long and passionate congratulatory kiss. When the restaurant broke into applause and whistles they held each other and kept kissing as if they were all alone.

Soon, Press and Helen and their baby boy celebrated their new union with an enormous wedding. Press Maravich's teammates and dozens of sailors and airmen were in attendance to witness their charismatic friend take the marital plunge.

In the late 1940's, spending $7,000 on a wedding was an extraordinary amount of money for most people. The Maravich-Montini wedding included seven groomsmen and seven bride's maids. During the reception there was big band music, dancing and a collection of funds from his friends that paid all of the wedding costs. Soon, a new baby boy that Press wanted to name "Peter Maravich," would be on his way. On June 22, 1947, Peter Maravich was born. And on that day, there was one man who knew beyond the shadow of any doubt that the newborn bearing his namesake would change the game forever.

"I knew the minute I saw Pete that I was looking at a child who could grow up to be the greatest basketball player the world had ever seen!" Press declared.

"How did you know, Press?

"I just did," Press shrugged.

CHAPTER 12
True Legends Are Created

How could a man look at his newborn baby in a crib and make such an outlandish remark? Perhaps Press was hoping, or maybe he experienced a spiritual premonition?

Press Maravich held his baby boy and he said to the delivering doctor that Peter Maravich would grow into one of the greatest basketball players to ever play the game. Think of the millions of proud dads and moms who have cuddled their newborn and dreamed of the child's future. Perhaps they envisioned a future for their son in the National Basketball Association.

When my wife, Pamela, and I studied the sonogram of our first baby and discovered he was a boy I have to admit that I immediately thought how fun it would be to play baseball with little Casey! When he was old enough to stand I set out to help Casey Jack (named after my dad) become the best pitcher and shortstop I could. He was a standout shortstop, pitcher and hitter. Because he was raised watching *Pistol Pete Homework Basketball* videos Casey learned to dribble beautifully and shoot from anywhere.

When my second son, Brock, was born, I had the same notions. He played football, basketball and developed a love for baseball, becoming an outstanding pitcher, infielder and hitter. My daughter, Addy, played on a traveling softball team and became a point guard who could drain a three-pointer from about anywhere on the court. Her high school basketball team won a state championship.

My youngest son, Brett, has patterned his game after "Pistol Pete." He has developed terrific fundamentals with either hand, behind the back and between the leg passes and proficient shooting from all ranges on the court. He now plays on the college level.

It's no surprise that my time spent with my sports idol influenced the way Pam and I raised our competitive children.

"We are looking forward to starting a family," I told Pete back in 1985.

"Are you and Pam old enough to have kids? You look like a kid yourself," Pete joked.

"I'm twenty-eight."

"You look like you're sixteen," Pete laughed. "You'll be able to get a student discount when our movie comes out."

"I'll sneak in. I refuse to pay," I laughed.

"I'm convinced that I could have been a much better athlete if I had my spiritual life together. When I played I was just playing for myself, or maybe my dad. I wish I could have said I was playing for God and not myself," Pete shared with some regret in his voice.

"Are you saying you could've scored more points or played better if you had been a Christian?"

"I know I could have. I mean, I was having fun doing what I was doing but I think my head would have been clearer and I would have been more focused."

"You averaged forty-four points a game in college," I jokingly reminded him.

"Should have been more."

"You still have the record for most games scoring fifty or more points."

"I know I could have had more. I'm convinced."

"You still have the record for most free throws."

"Because I always had two or three guys on me, hacking me!" Pete laughed. "It just made me better."

"You made thirty out of thirty-one attempts against Oregon State."

"I can still see that one shot I missed. I don't know how that happened!"

Pete was recalling the night he set the all-time record for most free throws made in a game. In his voice, I could hear the frustration as he wished he could go back in time and shoot that one shot again.

"I was a basketball android, Darrel. That's all I wanted to do—play basketball. I had three goals in my life: become a professional basketball player, be the first player to be paid a million dollars to play basketball, and win a championship ring so I could wear it and prove that I was one of the greatest players ever to play. That free throw record should be thirty-one out of thirty-one."

The word "legend" is often overused, but in the case of a few athletes it is appropriate. In the past, a folk tale, saga or myth would be referred to as a "legend." These days, we hear men and women referred to as "film legends," "sports legends" and "military legends." Words such as "icon," "phenomenon," "megastar" or "celebrity" are used in our culture when one is referring to noteworthy people.

Dozens of writers and sports commentators have referred to "Pistol Pete" as a legend. They often refer to his exploits on the basketball court as legendary, because even the most accomplished wordsmith in sports finds it challenging to put into sentences what Pete did on the court.

One of the many reasons I've come to enjoy websites like YouTube is that people who never witnessed Pete playing, or those who forgot the uniqueness and excitement of the way he played can now watch and not rely on hearsay or hyperbole.

In my travels around the country, I often encounter fortunate sports enthusiasts who had the privilege of watching "Pistol Pete" play in person. They often use the word "legend" which led to our decision to subtitle *The Pistol: Birth of a Legend*.

Our reasoning for the subtitle was our attempt to demonstrate through the film that there was a mythical beginning to Pete's journey that bordered on folklore due to the oral history perpetuated through the years.

Fortunately, his basketball records speak for themselves. I have recently heard of people watching old LSU games and trying to calculate how many points Pete would have scored if the three-point line had been in existence. When Pete told us that Press had shot sixteen-millimeter footage of every one of Pete's games in college, Frank and I felt as though we had been handed a treasure map.

"Where is the footage?"

"It's in the attic," Pete replied nonchalantly. "There wasn't video tape like today, so my dad got someone to stand up in the top of the arena and film every game."

This is a good time in this book to pause and remind the reader of some of the basketball records Pete Maravich broke or still holds after playing his three years at Louisiana State University. Most "Pistol Pete" fans are acutely aware of the impact Maravich had on collegiate basketball from 1966-70, but a quick immersion into Pete's accomplishments can be both enlightening and perhaps inspiring.

To say that Pistol Pete Maravich made a "mark" on basketball is a gross understatement. Many writers have to lean on hyperbole to explain Pete's phenomenal rise to greatness. It's fun to list just some of his accomplishments so readers can enjoy the quick "snap shot" of history. Here are a few of the college facts:

1. All-Time NCAA Career Scoring Leader with record 3,667 points. (3 years; no three-point line)
2. Record average of 44.2 points for 83 games.
3. Ranks first, fourth and fifth in NCAA history for most points in a single season.
4. Averaged a record 43.8 points per game in 1968.
5. Averaged a record 44.2 points per game in 1969.
6. Averaged a record 44.5 points per game in 1970.
7. Scored 69 points vs. Alabama, Feb. 7, 1970.
8. Led LSU to the NIT Final Four in 1970.
9. First-team All-American in 1968.
10. First-team All-American in1969.
11. First-team All-American in 1970.
12. Naismith Award winner in 1970.
13. Sporting News College Player of the Year 1970.
14. The Sporting News All-America First Team 1968.
15. The Sporting News All-America First Team 1969.
16. The Sporting News All-America First Team 1970.
17. AP and UPI First-Team All-America 1968.
18. AP and UPI First-Team All-America 1969.
19. AP and UPI First-Team All-America 1970.
20. NCAA record for most field goals made: 1,387.
21. NCAA record, most field goals attempted: 3,166.
22. NCAA record for most free throws made: 893.
23. NCAA record most free throws attempted: 1,152.

24. NCAA record for most games scoring at least 50 points. 28 games.

25. NCAA single-season record for most points: 1,381.

26. NCAA highest per game average of 44.5 points per game in 1970.

27. Ranks 1st, 4th and 5th for most points in a single season.

28. NCAA single-season record for most field goals made with 522.

29. NCAA single-season record for most field goals attempted: 1,168 field goals in 1970.

30. Holds NCAA single-season record for most games scoring with at least 50 points. Ten games in 1970.

31. Holds NCAA single-game record for most free throws made. 30 of 31 against Oregon State on Dec. 22, 1969

32. Averaged 43.6 points per game on the LSU freshman team in 1967. Not eligible for varsity.

33. Scored 66 points vs. Tulane - Feb. 10, 1969

34. Scored 64 points vs. Kentucky - Feb. 21, 1970.

35. Scored 61 vs. Vanderbilt (Dec. 11, 1969)

36. Holds LSU record for most field goals in a game. 26 against Vanderbilt on Jan. 29, 1969

37. Holds LSU record for most field goals attempted in a game. Fifty-seven (57) points against Vanderbilt.

38. All-Southeastern Conference 1968.

39. All-Southeastern Conference 1969.

40. All-Southeastern Conference 1970.

In 1988, Louisiana Governor Buddy Roemer signed legislation that changed the official name of Louisiana State University's basketball arena to the Pete Maravich Assembly Center.

"My dad wasn't looking around for a rebuilding job," Pete explained. LSU hadn't had any excitement in their programs since the 1950s, back when Bob Pettit was playing, so Pop was sure he could do something positive for the Tigers."

"Where did you want him to coach?"

"Anywhere in the Atlantic Coast Conference (ACC). But Dad was always in debt, and taking the job in Baton Rouge would help the family. The man who hired Pop, Jim Corbett, passed away suddenly before Dad showed up in Louisiana, so one of his new assistant coaches, Jay McCreary, showed him around the campus. That was the first time my dad saw the Cow Palace."

Coach McCreary showed Press around campus, which included the arena where Press would debut, his first LSU Tiger team. The arena was used for almost anything but basketball. Press was informed that a horse show would have the dirt-floored arena until two weeks before his first game.

"My dad was used to making something out of nothing. It reminded me of when he was a kid and a pastor helped him build a court at his church," Pete recalled. "At Davis and Elkins College, they didn't even have a dirt floor livestock arena like at LSU. They had nothing."

"Nothing?" I quizzed.

"My dad borrowed a tractor and cleared an area of dirt by himself, and then he had the local newspaper run a story about Davis and Elkins breaking ground for a new gymnasium! He ended up getting a bunch of construction guys together to build it," Pete shook his head and laughed.

These are the kinds of stories that Pete and Press loved to tell. They are stories that are sometimes forgotten on the pages of history but components that help to make up the legends.

129

As a fan, we remember Coach Maravich on the LSU bench holding a towel to his mouth. That white towel in his hand and held to his face was one of Press's trademarks. We also remember the iconic picture of Press standing in front of the Tigers bench watching as "Pistol Pete" is hoisted onto the shoulders of his teammates after he broke Oscar Robertson's college scoring records. What we forget is the disastrous start for Press when Pete was a freshman and not eligible to play for his dad's varsity squad.

Despite Press informing the newspapers and alumni that he had brought a superstar to the school, the community and LSU fans around the country were still focused on their football team. Football was all that really mattered to most Tiger fans. When the first basketball season concluded, Press and his varsity team struggled to a predictable 3-23 record.

Meanwhile, Pete and the freshman team were causing a stir. There had never been a ball-handler, passer, or shooter like the new freshman guard and soon the word was out that if LSU fans wanted to enjoy watching basketball on campus they should attend the freshman games to see the new coach's kid, Pete Maravich. Pete had grabbed the immediate attention of the students when he scored fifty points in his first game.

"It was pretty simple; what happened," Pete continued. "I just put on a show and made believers out of the skeptics. I was a skinny kid from North Carolina who only knew one way to play—up-tempo. At first, the fans weren't anticipating much, but I was determined to get them hooked and show them how Dad and I believed basketball should be played."

In a matter of a few games Pete began a shift in the athletic program. The shift wasn't from football to basketball, but there was an exciting new addition to the athletic department at LSU.

130

Rather than sparse crowds and empty seats, the "Cow Palace" was sold out for the freshman games. Before long, Pete's remarkable play in the Southeastern Conference was the subject of much of the sports world. As the varsity struggled to accomplish their 3 wins, the Baby Bengals were stacking up seventeen straight victories.

"After our freshman game and before my dad's varsity game, campus security was busy directing traffic away from the arena. I wish that was a joke, but it's the truth," Pete said. "People didn't want to sit through a varsity game."

"How about the legend of your floppy socks?"

"I was going to play one night and I'd forgotten my socks. I borrowed some old worn-out gray work socks without any elastic in them. They drooped down around my ankles and over my shoes."

"Did you ever think that it would start a fashion fad?"

"Honestly, it happened because I hated my big feet. I thought they looked too big, and I was self-conscious. So, when I saw those socks covering up part of my shoes I thought it made my feet look smaller, and I thought it made me a little faster," Pete chuckled. "It was all in my mind, but I kept wearing them, and the floppy socks became a trademark."

"A good luck charm?"

"Not really. Maybe I thought they were at the time."

The other legendary trademark was "Pistol Pete's" hair.

"I really liked Joe Namath. He was such a maverick and didn't care what people thought about him. He also played football like he was having a lot of fun," Pete explained.

"Most guys your age had short hair. Did you grow it long to be different?" I asked.

131

"It was because of Namath. I had long hair like his, but mine was straighter like the style the Beatles had made popular in the early 1960s."

Pete continued to explain where he was emotionally, and he wanted to talk about his lack of maturity after the freshman year. Although the team had won seventeen in a row, all he could think about was how he had missed the back end of a two free-throw opportunity.

"I couldn't believe it. I made the first one and the second shot rolled around the rim and fell out. I can still picture it in my mind," Pete complained.

That was the night that Pete left the locker room and walked two miles back to the hotel without telling anyone. Losing was always difficult for Pete to accept.

I've already listed many of the accomplishments that Pete experienced during his time in college, and writing another detailed biography about Pete isn't what this book is about.

I had the amazing privilege of spending many days with Pete and Press as I wrote *Heir To A Dream*, and author-biographers such as my friends Wayne Federman and Marshall Terrill, who wrote *Maravich*, covered many of the facts that make up the legends surrounding Pete. My goal is to continue sharing with you the personal events we shared and the candid conversations that happened exclusively with Pete, Press and me during our years together. Meeting, interviewing, and befriending Pete was the culmination of years of trying to imitate my hero. When I was in junior high school in Missouri, it was the genesis of "Pistol Pete" beginning to affect my life and my friends' lives as well as impacting our view of basketball. In the late 1960s, high school kids started wearing floppy socks and tried to pass between their legs and behind their backs like Pete.

As in our movie, *The Pistol: The Birth of a Legend,* I witnessed kids being reprimanded by some coaches for playing "showboat" basketball. While watching *The Pistol,* audiences can get a glimpse of old-style, traditional basketball as it began to clash with the new styles of play Pete helped introduced. One reporter called Pete the "Elvis of basketball" because he truly revolutionized the game. With the help and encouragement of his dad, Pete's run-and gun shooting, no-look passing, and deceptive dribbling were unleashed upon the public.

"If you got a good horse, you run him!" Press told me.

I think of Press every time I notice a basketball coach pull the "hot hand" shooter out of the game.

"When a player is "on fire" and in his rhythm, you keep him on the floor, not on the bench!" Press grumbled. "When you have your opponent down, you put your foot to the pedal! Don't ever let up." Press scowled, "I wanted Pete to score a hundred in a game if it was possible. Isn't putting the ball through that iron circle what it's all about?"

Sometimes, reducing things to the ridiculous is the best way to succeed. For Press, it was the best way to approach the game.

"Pete was a great shooter because I taught him to shoot properly and because he practiced shooting properly all his life," Press explained.

Pete reminded me, "I tell kids in my *Homework Basketball* camps, *If the kid reads a book ten times and I read that same book one thousand times, which one of us is going to know the book better?*"

"The person who reads the book a thousand times."

"It's the same with shooting a basketball. I lived with a basketball under my arm or in my hands."

"You always carried a ball?"

133

"Always. I used to go to the old movie theater in Clemson and watch a matinee. If nobody else sat nearby I would dribble my basketball in the aisle while I watched the movie. I dribbled my basketball as I rode my bike to school. I carried it in the hallway at school. I sneaked out of class to get a few quick shots in the gym. You should put that in the movie," Pete smiled.

"I made that note already," I assured him.

"One time I snuck out of class. I told the teacher I was sick or something and then I went down to the gym, and my coach came in and found me skipping class."

"What did he say?"

"He made me run laps. I don't think he cared. He knew I loved the game and that I was just trying to get better," Pete explained. "I was totally motivated. I would wake up in the morning, like when I was eleven or twelve years old, and the first thought on my mind wasn't like most kids. You know, *What's for breakfast? Where's my Cheerios?* The first thing on my mind was, someone out there in the world my age is practicing more than me, and there are only so many college scholarships to go around."

"Are you serious? You were afraid someone was going to get your scholarship?"

"That's how I was wired. That was my thinking. My dad gave me that speech about not being able to pay for me to go to college. I was young when he challenged me to practice and get better at fundamentals—better than anyone in the country. That was my motivation," Pete assured me.

Press told me during a phone call that he had to motivate Pete. Even at LSU, Press was encouraging Pete with creative dibbling and passing drills that could improve his game.

"You know how young guys get when they think they know everything," Press explained. "Being Pete's dad and his coach had some challenges that people don't realize. He and I got into it a few times right in public and during a game."

"What would Pete say in the huddle?"

"Sometimes he wanted to tell me what we should be doing or what offense or defense to run. Yes, he was the star player, but I was the coach and his dad. It's hard to explain if you've never been in that position."

"Most players will never understand that feeling."

"It's unique for sure. During a game I was coach and that was that. When Pete was practicing I didn't want him to ever relax on perfecting the fundamentals ... dribbling, passing and shooting correctly. I would get my assistant, Jay, to talk to Pete one-on-one and to give him some pointers that were actually from me," Press smiled coyly. "I told Jay to pretend that he thought up the new drill. He would give my new drill to Pete and I would watch out of the corner of my eye to see Pete working on the new drill that I had dreamed up," Press nodded with pride.

"Coach McCreary would give me a drill to do and I would do it over and over to work on my ball-handling, or whatever," Pete explained. "I'd get real good at it and then I'd say to Pop, *Hey, look what Coach taught me*, you know, like *Why don't you ever dream up some things like that, Pop*?"

Pete laughed, remembering how foolish he must have sounded to Press.

"I thought Coach McCreary was as good as my dad about coming up with all these great ideas, but it was my dad's wild imagination and his innovation all along. Ha! I should've known," Pete explained.

135

CHAPTER 13
North Hollywood Sessions

Although I hadn't labeled the audiotape, I could tell as I listened to it that Pete, Frank and I were sitting and talking in my living room in Studio City, California. Throughout the interview I could hear my baby boy, Casey, as he played with his toys. Sometimes the squeal of his voice overshadowed the conversation, but I could tell that Pete was used to the sounds of kids in the room. He never lost track of his thoughts and he would continue speaking through the baby jabbering. Just like when he played, "Pistol Pete" never took his mind off the task at hand.

By this time, Press had grown seriously ill with cancer and our book, *Heir to a Dream*, was completed. We agreed to return to the original objective, which was to position Frank to produce and direct a movie about Pete. The three of us relaxed in the living room of the one-bedroom apartment Pam and I rented on Aqua Vista Street in North Hollywood.

"So we're each in agreement that we are developing a family film that is focused on Pete as a boy?" I began the discussion.

"I want people to see something on the screen that they can relate to. I don't care if it was thirty years ago, if it still relates to what I'm going through today," Pete started.

"I like period movies, and if we set your story in say, the late 1950s, we'll get the vintage cars and the soda shop look. You know, like the old style basketball uniforms with the silky shorts and the belt with a buckle," I laughed. "That's what my teammates and I wore in junior high."

136

Frank loved the idea and was already thinking about how he would direct the film. He wanted to shoot the soda shop scene with Pete spinning the ball and winning the bet against his friends. Frank and my good friend, Rodney Stone, talked with Dr. Pepper who agreed to provide product placement merchandise for the film as well as apparel for the production crew. Champion Sports agreed to create vintage basketball uniforms. The uniforms worn by the actors in our low budget sports movie turned out to be as authentic as any Hollywood studio wardrobe department could have created.

"Pete, let's get into your junior high life so I can flesh out the character in the movie. When you think back to those days as a thirteen-year-old, what do you remember about yourself?" I continued.

"I was a basketball android. I hated school. The classroom intimidated me. I feared failing in the classroom," Pete said without hesitation.

"That's something most kids can relate to, I think," I assured Pete.

"I didn't study much. I didn't fail, but I was so shy. I would have to get up in front of the class to give a report and I was afraid the kids would give me a hard time. I hate the way kids treated other kids in junior high—very poisonous individuals. I had a teacher named Miss Stanley. She had a big paddle."

"Did she use it?"

"That's why she had it. See, I was one of those kids who would cheat and look on other kid's papers for answers. I was fast and I would get away with it. One time, Miss Stanley called my name. She thought that I was cheating. I wasn't cheating, but she thought I was."

"What happened?"

"It was like that TV show, *Paper Chase*. Professor Kensington? You're full of fear and afraid that he'll call your name. They were all great actors in that show. You ever watch it?"

"I saw a few episodes," I replied.

"If you ever get a chance to see that show, it's great—all the conflict and the ego and all the greed. It's a great series and John Houseman is just tremendous. When I watched it I was scared. Whose he gonna call on?"

"Like Miss Stanley?" I asked trying to get Pete back on track.

"She thought I was cheating so she took me to the principal. The school called Mom and Dad and when they came in she accused me. I told them I wasn't cheating. And then I cried. Pop was upset but Mom was cooler about it. I had to wait until after class and when all the kids were gone and I just sat there waiting. She went through her purse and cleaned her desk as I sat there. Finally, she got that big old paddle and she was a big lady! I had to bend over the desk and she let me have it. Bam! That was it."

"Nowadays she might go to jail," I laughed.

As much as I loved the idea of that story being a scene, we didn't put it in the movie.

In order to show what Pete's grade school environment was like, I included a scene of Pete standing in front of his class reading an English paper. He states how he wanted to play professional basketball and become the first million-dollar player. He concludes the speech by saying he wants to win a championship ring to prove he was one of the best in the world. Adam Guier, the boy we cast as Pete in the movie, did an outstanding job performing the nervousness as described.

In an eighth grade classroom environment, Pete was stifled and nervous, the very opposite of his demeanor while playing a basketball game.

"When I was twelve I wanted to play basketball in the pros. I didn't care about Christopher Columbus and learning things about history. I mean, I know that learning your cultural heritage and where you came from is important or you'll lose your nation. You have nothing to fall back on. I didn't care about all that back then."

"What else do you remember about school?"

"You know, I was real skinny," Pete paused to remember. "I had a locker full of papers and books and I'd open the door and it would all fall out. Lunch was great—lunch and recess. I hated the classroom."

If we hoped to make a film for young people that might somehow encourage them to study hard, this story of a young "Pistol Pete" was not going to serve us in that regard. It was clear by now that Pete only had one main thing on his mind in the eighth grade and that was basketball. We tried another angle.

"What about your friends, Pete?

"Lou Riley."

"Boo Riley? Like in *To Kill a Mockingbird*? I kidded.

"No. 'Lou.' Lou was big … he could wipe us all out. I would tease him and light him up and then I'd run away. Lunch, physical education and recess were all great because we'd play football, and we put Lou on our team. He wasn't dumb, but he was uncoordinated. He was six-feet-two inches tall and he would say whatever you wanted him to say, or do whatever you said to do. I knew just how far to push him before he killed me and then I'd run off."

As Pete recounted the story he stood up and limped around the room like Frankenstein's monster. He flailed his arms and drug one foot across the floor.

"If you want to make this an R-rated thriller, you could have Lou go on a rampage at the end of the film and he would kill all us kids on the playground for picking on him. Arrrrrrgh!" Pete growled as he walked in a tight circle.

We laughed hysterically as Pete flopped back into his chair to continue his story.

"Ouch, that hurt my shoulder," Pete winced and laughed. "But it was worth it to tell you the story, I guess. It's the truth! There was another kid named Danny that nobody messed with because he was a fighter. I didn't want any part of that guy. One day we got in a fight and I kicked him in the privates or he kicked me."

"Wait! How do you forget that?" I asked Pete as we laughed.

"I don't remember. Anyway, Danny was walking around all cool. He was strong, but I fought him, and a teacher ran over and stopped us. She said, 'I'll see you after class.' We got five swats."

"Did the kids pick on you because you were so little?"

"Usually, because of who I was the kids didn't bother me. I was coming into my own as a star athlete and they respected that," Pete remarked as he pivoted back to the previous thought. "Hey, if you put Lou in the movie, that's a winner."

"Any other friends?"

"I hung around with the guys who were a year older than me. I wasn't the kingpin … Johnny, Ed, Matt, and Bunny; we hung around each other.

"What about girls?"

"I had crushes all time, and if I had my eye on a girl I would hope I would get in the same class with her. Just sitting by a girl in the classroom was enough. I had a crush on a girl who was eventually the runner-up in the Miss South Carolina beauty contest. She liked me, too. There was a girl named Reba who tried to get us together, but I was too scared and very withdrawn. Miss South Carolina married Stanley.

Did you go to dances in junior high?"

"We had dances, but I didn't want to go. I mean, I wanted to, but I told that girl who had the crush on me that I didn't want to go. It didn't help that I didn't know how to dance with a girl and I always thought that I would step on her feet. My feet grew faster than my body. Maybe I wasn't that clumsy. Maybe it was more in my mind because I was so shy that I didn't know how to act in those situations. I didn't want to be rejected. I was physically immature and girls at that age are more developed."

"I don't think it was clumsiness. You weren't clumsy on the basketball court."

"I could use basketball as an excuse. I didn't give her the time of day, and I was really stupid. She was good looking! All the girls I liked were good looking. I thought about girls but I just didn't know what to do about it. One day I got in trouble for dropping my pencil because I was trying to look under the desk at a girl. The teacher told my dad and Pop scolded me and said, *Pete, you are a really weird kid*, Pete laughed.

"Let's talk about your Mom. What was Helen like when you were twelve?"

Pete launched in to a description of his mother and I noticed that each time he talked about her the tone in his voice changed to melancholy laced with pride.

"She was the best," Pete nodded.

Pete bragged about her consistency in his life during his youth. He honored Helen, and throughout my days spent with Pete he often repeated that fact.

"She was always there for me," Pete reminded.

He wanted to make it clear that an actress who would take a gentle and caring approach to the role should play Pete's mother in the film.

"Mom was always there when I was crying and upset. She was there. Always tender, no matter what. When I fell down the steps, she was there."

The angst in Pete's voice was heartbreaking. It was as if he wished he could bring her into the room to prove how sweet and caring she was.

"That time when my brother hit me with a brick, she was there. The world says it isn't cool, getting kissed and hugged by your mom, but that's how she was. Dad was tough. Dad was never around. What I mean is; he was gone quite a bit. Ronnie was a teenager, off doing his thing. I was young and I would be home with my mother. Saturday mornings we were the only ones at the house. Mom was the perfect housewife, never complaining. In the movie it would be okay to show my mom complaining that Dad was never home."

The tape I was listening to ended abruptly and I stopped transposing Pete's words onto my computer screen. It was then I was reminded of how much Pete enjoyed reminiscing about Helen. The pain he suffered from the loss of his mother was overshadowed by the love she had given him in his youth. The sweet memories he carried into adulthood sustained him.

CHAPTER 14
Coming to Terms

We were in Baton Rouge when we visited the post office and retrieved the first handful of envelopes from customers who wished to buy Pete's new basketball instructional video series. Long before the Internet could market a product, Frank advertised in a few sports publications announcing to basketball enthusiasts that there was a new instructional tape called *Pistol Pete's Homework Basketball*.

The sales were brisk and ESPN promoted the product on the air and in their publications. Videos and videotape players were relatively new in people's homes at that time. We used to laugh because Frank's videotape player in his house was the size of a carry-on suitcase. We joined a long list of pioneers in the industry of instructional videos as Frank and I were recognized at an awards gala at the Roosevelt Hotel in Hollywood for our work on *Homework Basketball*.

About that same time, our book *Heir to a Dream* was about to be printed and sent to bookstores across the nation. The publisher expected Pete's story to be a big seller. The only cloud hanging over the release of the book project was Press and his illness. He was happy that the book was finished and that the *Homework Basketball* video was being produced, but his health was failing so fast that we all were afraid he wouldn't get to see our work in its completed form. His condition constantly tempered our exuberance.

I often thought of how different things would have been had Press been healthy and had been able to help us produce *Homework Basketball* and promote *Heir to a Dream*. After all, no one pushed the attributes of "Pistol Pete" like Press.

An enjoyable part of creating and videotaping *Homework Basketball* was paying homage to two of basketball's greatest players and innovators. I had already written into the movie script notes that I wanted a scene of Press coaching and instructing his Clemson Tigers team. Frank and I knew that it would take a terrific actor to interpret the thoughts and actions of Press and after having worked with actor Nick Benedict on the soap opera *Another Life*. We came to the same conclusion that Nick was perfect for the role.

This basketball represents everything there is to learn about the game. The small circle is what I know about the game. This tiny dot in the circle is what you know, Press would bark at his players. *If you'll forget about the cars and the girls, you might just learn something!*

The Pistol: Birth of a Legend movie features Press admonishing his players with that speech. Nick Benedict truly delivered an excellent performance during that scene and it is still one of my favorites.

"I'm going to do whatever I have to do to save my dad's life," Pete told me with conviction. "I'm looking into some experimental cancer treatment in Germany and I'm going to get him over there if it's the last thing I do."

Pete felt as though he owed it to Press to search anywhere across the world in order to find a cure for his father's cancer. Pete was willing to pay any price to help relieve the pain and suffering. Most of all, he would try any experimental drug or treatment known at the time.

"I owe everything to my dad," Pete continued. "His dream was to push the boundaries of basketball and he had trained me to stretch the game for him, for us, and for fans everywhere."

Pete confessed he needed to apologize to his dad, but he felt he couldn't do it until he got his life straightened out. He needed Press to forgive him for all the times he "messed up."

"Dad had a chance to win a national title at the NIT (National Invitational Tournament), but he didn't know that I had blown the championship game for him because I had been out all night before the big game."

"It had been over a decade, but I had to apologize to Pop for destroying his one chance at a championship. I simply told him, *I'm sorry. I stayed up all night drinking in New York and I was no good for you that night.*"

"How did Press respond to your apology?" I prodded.

"He was uncomfortable at first. He didn't want to have to deal with it. I had to force him to truly consider what I was trying to say to him. I had blown LSU's chance at a national title and I know it really messed up my Dad's career. He always acted as if it were no big thing and wanted to move on, but I told him that I wasn't leaving his bedside until everything was right between us. He said, 'Okay, I forgive you.'"

Until that serious moment between father and son, Press admitted that he had always blamed himself for the loss in New York. It was after the act of forgiveness that Pete explained to his dad that he was once where Press was; full of bitterness and hurt from all the things that had gone wrong in their lives. Press had suffered through his wife's alcoholism and tried desperately to raise Pete's little sister on his own. Being fired from his coaching job at LSU was another wound that hadn't healed.

"I told Pop that every sin anyone ever committed was forgiven through Christ's death."

"How was that received by him?"

"Honestly, Pop had a difficult time believing that God could forgive him for all the things he had done wrong in his life. I told him that God loves him anyway. We don't go to hell because of the sin. Jesus paid for that on the cross. We are separated eternally from God because we fail to believe. I didn't see a need for Jesus in my life until I was at the end of the line. Nothing was fulfilling. I had money, fame and material possession, but I didn't have happiness. You can look for happiness all your life and never find it, but when you find Jesus and accept him, happiness finds you."

"Did Press become a Christian at that time?"

"It was a few years later," Pete continued. "Pop saw that what I believed was a real thing with me and long term, not just another religious search or phase I was going through. Pop went to a church service one night and at the end of the preacher's message the pastor had an alter call. Actually, it took about three attempts, but the preacher persisted, saying that he was convinced that there was someone in the church that night that needed to ask the Lord into their life. Well, he was right. My dad finally walked down the aisle of the church and that was the night he became a committed believer in Jesus. After that experience, he was a different person. All the bad thoughts of the past that had haunted him were gone and he really enjoyed some peace."

"After all those years of basketball conversations, you two had something else that connected you."

"That's right. We talked about eternity all the time."

"What about your mother? Was that too difficult for you two to talk about?"

"You never totally get over something like that. Before it happened, Pop was fired from Louisiana State, and he had never been out of a job or been fired."

146

"I didn't realize he was fired," I said, revealing my ignorance regarding that part of Pete's life.

"Oh, yes. It was a shock. It came at a terrible time for Mom. The 1971-72 season was really a rough, losing season for the Tigers and they let him go. He panicked. Pop threw himself in to the first job he could find and that was at Appalachian State. I couldn't believe it when he told me. I wanted him to continue on the major college level because his basketball mind was as good as any coach out there."

"He could have landed a job coaching in several other major universities, couldn't he?" I asked.

"Yes! That's what I was mad about. I begged him not to jump into another bad situation. My third year with the Hawks, Dad was having a miserable year at his new job. There was no money for the basketball program and the players had to drive their own cars to away games. Mom was unhappy and drinking and getting more depressed. Oh, yeah, and that's when I got Bell's palsy."

"What is that?"

"It's a paralysis of the face; one side of my face. I stepped off the team bus in New York City and my face went numb on one side. My right eyelid wouldn't shut. It really scared me because I had no idea what was happening.

"I've never heard of that."

"I was like you; I had never heard of Bell's palsy either. Doctors said it was a disease they didn't know much about and when I asked them how long I would be paralyzed they said they didn't know. One doctor said it might be a couple of years."

"Could you play ball with that condition?" I asked.

147

"I tried to play with goggles because my eye would dry out and burn really bad, Pete explained. "Thankfully, after a month it went away. Anyway, I'm just saying that there were a lot of negative things going on with my family at that time. You asked about Mom …"

"Yes. When did it happen? Or when did you find out?"

"My brother, Ronnie, called me. I knew something was up by the sound of his voice. Then, he said, 'Pete, Mom is in critical condition … she shot herself in the head.'"

I told Pete how very sorry I was, took a pause, and then asked him how he reacted to the shocking news.

"At first, I just couldn't believe it. I refused to believe it. I told Ronnie I would take off and be there as soon as possible. I packed a few things and tossed them in the car. I'll never forget that ride to the airport. I begged God to keep my mom alive for me. I was so angry with her for doing it. I just kept crying out, 'Why? Why?' At that time I didn't have a relationship with God, but I kept praying: 'Please, God, keep her alive.'"

"Did you make it back in time to see her?"

"When I arrived at the airport to catch a plane to Charlotte, I stopped and made a call from a pay phone."

"How's Mom?" Pete asked Ronnie.

"She didn't make it, Pete. Mom's dead," Ronnie told Pete as he stood in the busy airport.

I hated to have Pete recount the horrible night he learned about the death of his mother. It was obvious to me as he relayed the events of the night that although many years had passed since her tragic death, for Pete it was as if it were yesterday. The tone of his voice was full of as much remorse as it was sadness.

148

"Dad looked for help everywhere he could. He took Mom to hospitals, psychiatrists, counselors; anyone he thought might give her some help. But nothing helped. I was so mad!" Pete clinched a fist. "I wanted to punch something or just scream."

Pete recalled how his body felt numb as the news sunk in. Suddenly, a rush of memories of his mother hit him in waves: the way she cheered from the stands for him as a boy, the day she encouraged him to go out and shoot baskets with Press, the Christmases, the birthdays, and most Saturdays that Pete and Helen spent together.

Press was an admirer of everything he could teach his son to do on the basketball court, but Helen was his most devoted fan. She came to every game when he was young. She was the loudest mother in the stands. Pete told me Helen was "rah, rah." That was his way of saying she was very enthusiastic and into every basketball move he made. Yes, he played for his father, and he entertained his fans, but he played as if he were giving presents to his mother. He wanted to give her moments of happiness because he knew how proud she was of him, and during her darkest days Pete's accomplishments on the court brought her joy. Playing was his gift to her.

As Pete hung up the telephone, the only face he could envision was that of his healthy, loving, and compassionate mother. His heart was shattered. He wanted to wrap his arms around her and tell his hurting mother that everything would be okay. He longed for her voice and her words of encouragement, but alcohol abuse had robbed him and his entire family. It had taken the dedicated wife, loving mother and constant advocate out of the family picture forever. Pete felt robbed—violated. Her life had been stolen from them.

149

"I blamed myself. I had selfishly removed myself from her life and her struggles. I was so focused on my basketball career that I shoved everything else aside, including a close relationship as an adult with my mother."

"You were pursuing a dream she wanted for you."

"But I had made basketball my god and for the longest time I believed that the game could be the cure-all for any ill I had. With the death of my mother, I realized it couldn't cure anything. When I look back, I see that what my mother wanted more than anything was to be loved and cared for. Dad and I had spent so much time away from the woman who loved us and the loneliness took its toll on her. I think I put too much hope in the fact that Dad was trying to get her help. I figured someone would help her as I was off chasing my dream. I was wrong."

"What would you tell someone who is in that position today?" I asked.

"I would say to love the person and understand that alcohol is a demonic thing that can get a foothold and control in someone's life. Fight to get them help. If you care, fight like you've never fought before. I felt so sorry for my dad. Since my sister was two years old, my dad had been trying to coach major college basketball, raise a baby, and at the same time care for his wife who was inebriated most days. When he did leave for a while, he would come back home just hoping that my little sister was okay. Things got really bad and Pop didn't want to leave her alone with Mom. Like I said, I was so focused on myself that I put some of his struggle out of my mind."

"How did Press cope with what happened?"

"He was devastated."

"I had no idea, Pete. I'm sorry."

"I was sitting in the airport trying to get to him and all I could think of was embracing him and telling him that we would somehow make it through together. It was about one-thirty a.m. when I got to Boone, North Carolina."

Pete paused for a moment and then revealed to me a strange story that happened on his way to his parent's home that night. He was driving his rental car through mountain roads when an eighteen-wheeler big rig began riding his bumper behind him. Pete accelerated and tried to lose the aggressive driver, but it wasn't until he drove nearly 90 miles an hour that he was able to put some distance between him and the menacing trucker.

He was empty, scared, and upset from the harassment he received from the driver of the truck. He was shaking as his car pulled into the driveway. Before he could make it to the door Press came out of the house, strode toward Pete and they embraced each other. No words would come as they held each other in the darkness.

"All we could do was cry," Pete lamented.

That night was extremely long for Press and Pete. With Pete's sister asleep, the two men sat alone in the living room and tried to make sense of it all.

"When I left, she was sober," Press explained. "When I came home I found an empty whiskey bottle."

Pete explained that he believed his mother was beyond any rational thinking at the point of her death. He didn't believe it was premeditated in any way. In fact, Pete simply said, "I don't think that was my mother. She was someone else when she got that intoxicated. My mother wouldn't have taken her life like that. She loved us too much. She had become someone else, motivated by the alcohol."

That long and horrible night, Pete was consumed with guilt. The loving and open conversation that he and his father had through the early morning hours was what Pete longed for, but he wanted the conversation to be between his mother and him. But Helen was gone. As morning broke, Pete found himself staring at his mother's favorite chair. He imagined her walking into the room with a loving smile and welcoming him home.

"Hell is when you live eternity separated from God," Pete continued his painful story. "That's why there is darkness in hell. God isn't there. God is light and in him there is no darkness. I have prayed hundreds of times that my mother isn't separated from Him."

As Pete told me the story of his mother's passing, I knew his mind was consumed with the reality that his father was dying soon if he didn't receive exotic, experimental treatment for the bone cancer. It would be a last-ditch effort for life.

We agreed to take a break for the day. Telling me the details of the death of his mother was difficult for Pete. I knew there had to be hundreds of other gut-wrenching moments in the life of the Press Maravich family that dealt with Helen and her illness. Pete preferred to keep those things private, and so will I.

CHAPTER 15
An Unexpected Letter

On a perfect day in September, I walked to the row of
mailboxes at our apartment complex in North Hollywood. I
had been writing all morning, and as a discipline, I would
make myself stay in my office chair until I had reached the end
of a chapter. No matter what shape the chapter was in, I would
plow through to get to an ending so I could earn myself a moment to stand up and breathe. I had just reached the end of a
chapter of *Heir to a Dream*, and I felt satisfied as to how
things were progressing.

I jogged down the stairs, put my mailbox key into the
keyhole, opened the squeaky salmon-colored box, and noticed
an envelope sitting on its edge. The name "Press Maravich"
was typed on the front of the envelope. Press was more excited
about the development of the book, the instructional videos
and the movie than any of us. The pride he had in his son
combined with the fact that he was battling bone cancer provided a sense of urgency in his heart that pushed him to help
us get things completed.

I grabbed a letter opener, and cut open the envelope
from Press. I couldn't wait to see what he had written so I
could use some of his stories or insights in the book. In retrospect, I'm not sure if I used any content from his letter in *Heir
to a Dream*. As I recall, most of the story of *Heir* had been
written, and I was deep into the stories of Pete in college and
his impending entrance into the professional league.

When I decided to write this book, I searched through my filing cabinet full of papers and notes related to Pete and all the projects we did together. The files include the autobiography, the movie script drafts as well as a video project we created after Pete's death entitled *Maravich Memories*. When I came to a file folder that read "Press Maravich" on it, I flashed back to the day that envelope arrived in the mailbox in the fall of 1986.

Rather than sharing parts of the letter, I thought it would be entertaining for the reader of this book to get a real glimpse of Press and how his mind worked. The following is that letter verbatim:

Sept. 22, 1986
Hallelujah, Darrel,

It's about time you wrote, you lazy Hollywood star. Enjoyed your letter and your accolades because I am happy for God's glory that you enjoyed reading Two Minutes of Basketball *by The Pistol. I am sure that Pete would approve of it if you want to go ahead and change anything in* Two Minutes. *I'm sure you can add some extra dimensions to the book to make it more interesting.*

Diana (Pete's sister) is studying very hard on her Doctor's degree. She is also teaching freshman lab chemistry. That alone keeps her pretty busy preparing for her classes three times a week. She gets about $180.00 a month and that will be a big help in paying her rent, food, gas money and other incidentals. Besides, she is carrying a heavy load of Pharmaceutical Science courses.

I'm going to tell you something you won't believe. Last week, I went to the supermarket and there was a sale on for kosher pickles. I haven't eaten pickles in years.

So, I went ahead and bought a quart and in less than a week I ate all the pickles that were in the jar. You'd think I was pregnant or something. Don't laugh, Darrel, wait until your wife starts asking at 2:00 a.m. to run to the store and get her some pickles and ice cream. Yuk!

Trying to recall the '30s. My gosh, that is half a century ago. From 1933 to 1937, I played high school varsity basketball. I was the sixth man as a freshman. We played Braddock High School in Pittsburgh, Pa., on a Friday night – they were the Western Pennsylvania Interscholastic athletic league Champions the year before. I was sitting on the bench when the game started. It was the second game of the season. We had four seniors and a junior in the lineup. With less than two minutes to go in the game the coach called my name (believe me I was ready ... never let an opportunity slip by), and I went in for one of the seniors.

We were down two points. During those two minutes I swiped a pass, made a basket and later with only seconds to go, I made the winning field goal.

After the game the coach made me a starter and no one in my four years even came close to removing me from the lineup. I loved the competition too much to give up my starting role for the bench. I was even captain of the team for two years. Of course, later in life I coached my high school team.

1937 was my senior year. It was the second semester and I was looking forward to graduating. Also, those years in high school I worked in the steel mills in my hometown for the Jones & Laughlin Steel Corp. They were the fourth largest steel mill in the world at the time.

I lied about my age because we were all poor. At first they hired me as a laborer hooking up hot steel billets and sheet bar. Later on I got a promotion as a pipe threader at the Seamless Tube Mill. Pay was meager. At one time there were about 14,000 steel workers. Today, there are only 600, I'm told.

I worked from 11 p.m. until 7 a.m. sometimes four days or even five days a week. I went to class from 8:30 a.m. until 3:30 p.m.; practiced basketball from 3:30 to 5:30 p.m. Then I would rush for home where mother had my supper ready. I gulped everything down quickly then hit the sack for about four hours of shut-eye and then I'd get ready for the midnight shift again. It was rough, but as a youngster who didn't know any better I somehow managed.

Back to my second semester of my senior year in 1937 ... it was the first week of June we were in our final exams. My final was in English. It consisted of literature, poems; Shakespeare quotes, diagramming sentences, grammar and a 300-word composition. In the hallway, looking through the glass door, were two football players who were my good friends who were motioning for me to get them the exam and I kept moving my head in a "no way" fashion.

I was the first to get through with my exam and I gave it to my teacher, Miss Thiel. She said, "Well, it looks like you did a bit of studying for a change." I replied, "Yes, mam." I went back to my desk and started to open my biology book because that was the next exam for me. My two friends were still looking through the window. I tried to ignore them. They started to cross themselves, as both were Catholics. When the bell rang all the students started for Miss Thiel's desk and I joined the crowd.

When I got near the desk I slipped my left hand over the pile of exams and slipped one out. Then on the way out of class I told both of them not to make A's on the test because she will get wind of it. While I was in my biology class finishing my final exam, one of the students came in and asked Mr. Edeburn, our biology teacher, if Press Maravich could go see Miss Thiel.

So, I hopped over to see Miss Theil. When I entered her classroom I said, "Miss Thiel, did you want to see me?" she answered in a tone of voice that somehow made me uneasy. She said, "Where is your final exam paper?" I replied, "Miss Thiel, I was the first to hand in my exam." She said, "I know that, but your friends, Frank and Knute both made A's on their papers." I said, "It's possible they studied for a change. Are you sure there is no mistake somewhere?" She said, 'You want my honest opinion?' I shook my head yes. She said, 'Press, you are stupid. I think you stole your own exam by mistake and gave it to your friends.'

Anyway, I paid a dear price for stealing those exams of mine by mistake and believe it or not she failed me and passed the other two. I didn't speak to my friends for a long time. I went to summer school for four weeks and got an A.

Frank Hribar ended up as a football player at Duke Univ., and played pro ball with the Washington Redskins and after his playing days ran a bar in Norfolk, Virginia. Knute Gnup played and coached football in the Canadian league for about 15 years or so. Both of them died within a year of each other. I never did see them after we left school.

I had scholarships to Geneva College, Long Island University, Duquesne, Pitt and others. I ended up at Davis and Elkins College in Elkins, West Virginia because a friend of mine went there.

In my senior year in college ... 1941, I took up flying since the Navy was paying for it. I soloed and got a private pilots license. I didn't realize the full impact of that when I signed the agreement with the Navy because a guy with a little mustache was making all kinds of noise in Europe. I received a BA degree in Business Administration. I later, after the war years and after my pro years, went back to D. & E. as an assistant coach and got another degree in Health Education. So, I received two degrees from my alma mater – A.B.A. and a B.S. in Health Education. I was also the President of the Student Body.

The summer of 1941 I went back to my home and started working in the steel mill. I played pro ball that fall for the Clarksburg Pure Oilers. We played the Detroit Eagles who were the World Champs. I scored in the '30s and Dutch Denhert, who coached the Eagles—and who also invented the pivot play when he played for the Original Celtics—asked me if I would sign a contract with them. That I did on the spot. My first contract was for $4,000.

From September 7th to December 7th (Pearl Harbor Day) we played about 70 games. Then the Japs bombed Pearl and I received a telegram telling me to report to duty at the Anacostia, D.C. Naval Station. Up to now I've made many mistakes. That's what happens when one tries to hurry.

In all the years that I coached I was fired only once and that was from LSU, but I have forgiven them. My first big-time college ball as a coach was in the A.C.C (Atlantic Coast Conference) with the Clemson Tigers. My first or second game of the season some of the Clemson cadets at that time got inebriated and hung me in effigy. I was the first "Yankee" to be hung in effigy in the history of Clemson and I still hold that distinction today.

158

After I lost my job at LSU around 1971, I got a job with Appalachian State University. Pete was madder than a hornet. He thought I panicked. I found out later that Pete was right. The talent was not very good. So, I coached through a losing year. The following spring my wife was sick and it was in October of 1974 that she died. Anyway, I gave up my job and I got a job coaching in Sweden for a full year. I took my daughter and we put our house up for sale.

The change was good for the both of us. Diana was about 8 years old and we both studied the Swedish language. After one year we came back to the states and it was through Pete that I got the job as a professional scout with the New Orleans Jazz. I kept the job for about five years.

In 1982, I took a job with Campbell University and my daughter enrolled as a freshman. I was an assistant coach. I stayed at Campbell until 1985 and left. My daughter graduated in June 1986 and is back in school working on her Doctor's degree in pharmacology, which is an 8-year course.

For the past four years, Pete and I have been running a few summer basketball camps. Our summer basketball program is divided into three segments: Basketball, spiritual development and nutrition.

About my reaction when Pete left Boston: I never did know and never did ask Pete. The only thing I regret is that he didn't play with an outstanding center.

If you need any other information, write again.

May God Bless you and your family and keep all of you safe and in good health.

Because of Him,
"Press"
Press Maravich

I will always cherish that letter to me from Coach Maravich. Over the years I have taken it out of a file folder to read it and hear his distinct voice in my head. I'm glad to know it will now live in this book for readers to enjoy.

CHAPTER 16
Pete Back in Hollywood

Pete traveled to Los Angeles several times for business and to meet with me regarding the book and movie script. His visits to Hollywood became chapters of my life that will forever be etched in my memory. My childhood sports hero had become my writing, and business partner. But, most importantly, we had become friends who could work together and talk about anything.

For our second get-together in California, Pete came over to my apartment in North Hollywood. Pete ducked his head as he walked through our apartment doorway. Not that he was seven feet tall, but I'm sure the portal and the small apartment seemed confining compared to his beautiful home. He greeted my beautiful, pregnant wife and gave her a hug.

"So you're Miss Pam? How did you get so unlucky and marry this guy?" Pete laughed.

"Darrel stole me away from my high school sweetheart," she replied, never missing a moment to remind me.

It was a true statement of which I am proud.

"… And he brought you to La La Land from where?" Pete continued his inquiry.

"I grew up in Ashland, Missouri."

Like most people, not from mid-Missouri, Pete had never heard of the small town. Pam had grown up just south of Columbia, Missouri in Ashland with a population of just over one thousand residents in the 1980s. Pam and I met while she and I were attending Southwest Baptist College (now University).

I was a theater and English major and Pam was a psychology major and a pitcher on the fast-pitch softball team. To call Pam a "fish out of water" in Hollywood would be an understatement. She was a country girl from a tiny town and there were probably as many people living on our block in North Hollywood as there were living in her hometown.

"What's in Ashland?"

"Boone County High School."

"What's Ashland's claim to fame?" Pete continued as he took a seat on our couch.

"Pam was a hurdler and basketball player and she played on the softball team. That's probably it," I filled him in.

"I was a babysitter for Kate Capshaw's little girl," Pam interjected, knowing her relationship to Kate was her closest encounter with someone famous before joining the staff of *Days of Our Lives*.

"Who's Kate Capshaw?" Pete asked.

"She's an actress. Steven Spielberg's wife. Don't even ask me who Steven Spielberg is," I teased.

Pam explained that Kate had lived in Ashland for a while and that she had been the babysitter for Kate's girl, Jessica. Under the category of "it's a small world," Kate left the same small town of Ashland and later found fame as an actress in New York City. She married Spielberg while filming *Indiana Jones and the Temple of Doom*. Just a few months before Pete's visit, I had written an instructional video project that starred Kate as the host.

I'll never forget Kate's reaction when I walked up to her and introduced myself saying, "Hi, Kate. I'm Pamela Roger's husband."

"My babysitter in Ashland?"

That was probably the most obscure remark she had heard since becoming Steven Spielberg's wife.

"So, you're a small-town girl. Do you like it here?" Pete asked Pam.

"I love it; better than New York City where Darrel first dragged me to."

A few minutes later, we all walked into the kitchen to get a drink of water. Pam watched as Pete looked around the room. I noticed that she was glaring at me and I didn't know why. She later admitted that she hadn't thought of cleaning off the top of the refrigerator. We had never had anyone of Pete's height in our house before. To this day, Pam still thinks of cleaning off the top of the refrigerator before guests come to visit.

Pete opened the cupboard for a glass, and as people usually do in an unfamiliar kitchen, he opened a cabinet door that held our baking products instead of dishware. *Uh-oh*, I thought. *We are so busted.*

"This stuff will kill you, Pam."

And, so it began. Pete pulled a can of Crisco shortening out of the cabinet.

"You know what this stuff does to your veins?"

"Yes, I know, but I use it for my chocolate chip cookies. That's really all I ever use it for," Pam defended herself.

"Things like this that are solid at room temperature get clogged in your arteries. Like margarine."

Where had I heard that before?

"Pete, I have to inform you that my wife's chocolate chip cookies are legendary. When friends and relatives visit us, they ask if Pam will be cooking her famous chocolate chip cookies, so changing ingredients might never happen."

"I'm just saying this stuff will kill you."

"It's my Granny's recipe," Pam shrugged.

"Oh, sure. Blame poor Granny, huh?" Pete chuckled.

I had a new basketball I had secured for Pete to sign for our new baby, Pam, and me.

"Pete, will you sign something for me?"

"Sure."

I handed Pete the Spaulding Basketball that we had used during our *Homework Basketball* video series shoot. It's always a bit awkward getting a celebrity who is a friend to sign something for you, but in retrospect, I wish I would have had him sign basketball cards for all of my children as keepsakes.

My brother was a huge sports fan and card collector back in the day and he asked me to have Pete sign several basketball cards for his son, Brandon and him. I am so glad I did.

Because Pete left us so soon in his life, his personae and his accomplishments has made his personal memorabilia among the most highly sought-after collectibles in sports. In 2001, a used LSU jersey sold at auction for $94,300. The signed basketball from his sixty-eight point career high performance sold for $131,450 in 2009.

Pete would probably just smile if I could tell him these figures today regarding his memorabilia, especially the jersey he wore during that 1977 New York Knicks game. Trust me; Pete wouldn't care about the jersey. He would just want to focus on how, with one minute and eighteen seconds to go in the fourth quarter, the referee called an offensive foul on Pete as he drove in for a layup. Pete fouled out of the game and missed his chance at scoring seventy or more points. I apologize to my referee friends, including my son, Casey, but recently looked up that moment on YouTube. Pete had a good reason to be upset about that foul call.

"I should have been shooting free throws at the end of the game. I would've scored seventy points—maybe more!" Pete protested with some regret still lingering.

During this particular visit to Los Angeles, Pete was eager to get back onto a court and shoot some baskets. The thought of being in a gymnasium to watch Pete work out got Pam and me excited. Growing up in a state where the nearest pro team was the Kansas City Kings, nearly three hours away, I had never been near a professional basketball player.

"Do you guys know of a gym where I can go shoot?

"Our church has a gym," I informed him.

"Let's go," Pete replied with energy in his voice. It was clear that after all the years that had passed the prospect of his spending time in a gym shooting baskets could still bring him joy.

We laced up our sneakers and Pam, Pete, and I traveled to our church gymnasium in Van Nuys. I couldn't wait for Pam to see what I had witnessed months earlier in that gym in Fountain Valley.

Pam and I retrieved a couple of basketballs from a storage closet and brought them out on the court. I bounced one to Pete.

"Hey, Pam, did you play basketball in high school?"

"Yes, I was a point guard."

"I figured you weren't the center," Pete smiled.

Pam shook her head. She stands right at 5'3" in height.

"Let me see your shot."

Pam took aim and shot the ball from about fifteen feet away. The ball swished through the net.

"You have a nice shot, Pam."

"Thanks," Pam beamed.

Pam was thrilled to hear Pete tell her that her shot was "nice." Thirty-eight years later, if the moment bubbles up in conversation she still tells people that Pete Maravich told her she has a "nice shot."

"Count 'em, Pam," Pete encouraged as he began shooting his jump shot behind the three-point line.

Pete started in the left corner as I stood under the basket rebounding for him. Pete shot the ball and it swished the net. I threw the ball back to him, and he made shot after shot as he moved around the line.

Finally, after fifteen or more three-pointers, the ball hit the back of the rim and bounced back toward Pete.

"Ohhhhhh!" We collectively shouted as the ball bounced.

"That will NOT happen again!" Pete exclaimed.

"You'll never miss another shot?" I asked.

"I will never miss two in a row. Count 'em, Pam."

Pete started shooting again, and after about twenty shots the ball glanced off the back of the rim as before.

"Pamela!" Pete shouted.

We laughed as I fetched the ball and bounced it back to Pete.

"That will NOT happen again!" Pete shouted to Pam.

"Better not miss. She'll start doubting you."

"Guard me, Darrel," Pete challenged.

"Yeah, right ..." I replied, knowing that he was about to make a fool out of me.

"Guard me. I need a little pressure."

And like an idiot I walked out to the three-point line and Pete started dribbling.

"Try to get it."

166

I reached, but before I could even understand what was happening, the ball was behind him and he was dribbling with the other hand.

"Come on! Try!"

"I am trying!" I laughed.

Pete nearly broke my ankles as I tried to keep up with his moves. This was not the same player who walked away from the Celtics with tired legs and a weakened knee. He was truly amazing.

I've heard people compare Pete Maravich to a magician. I got to experience that trickery, deceptiveness, and humiliation first-hand. I thought Pete was going to pull up for a three-pointer as he had been doing for fifteen minutes. Instead, he dribbled between his legs and then between mine, took two strides, and he rolled the ball off his fingertips into the basket.

Pam laughed. Pete laughed. I shook my head and grinned. My regret was that I didn't have that hilarious and humiliating moment captured on camera to show my friends and my children today.

We spent an hour or so in that old gymnasium having the time of my life. I didn't care how stupid the legend made me feel, just being in Pete's presence brought joy to Pam and me. He treated us as if we were relatives whom he had known forever.

On a beautiful February morning in 1986, Pete had a photo shoot scheduled not far from Pam's office. Pam's job at the television studio was at Sunset-Gower Studios on Sunset Boulevard in Los Angeles. Pete gave me the address and asked me to meet him at the photo studio. I drove into Hollywood, parked my car on the street and walked to a four story building on Hollywood Boulevard.

167

Pete told me that the entrance was behind the building, and that I would have to walk through an alley and to the back door to find him. I carried a folded piece of paper in my pocket, and I pulled it out to make sure I was walking into the correct alley. The space between buildings was dirty and smelled of trash. As I made my way to the back door, I wondered what Pete had gotten me into.

The hinges on the back door squeaked as I opened it to the sporadic flashing of strobe lights in the photo studio. What I witnessed next would have thrilled most basketball fans. In front of a photographer's black backdrop was a group of basketball players dressed in white warm-ups with maroon logos. They were members of Meadowlark Lemon's Shooting Stars. I immediately recognized Curly Neal, Meadowlark, and Pistol Pete Maravich.

The shoot was wrapping up.

"Give me a few minutes to change and we'll get some lunch."

"Perfect," I told Pete.

I stood at the back door like I was a sports groupie waiting for autographs. After a few minutes, Pete walked out wearing blue jeans, a plain T-shirt, and new sunglasses.

"Hey, those sunglasses work for you here in Hollywood, Pete."

"Ya think?

"Of course! And out here, nobody cares who you are anyway," I teased.

"Thanks, Darrel," Pete sarcastically replied as he pointed toward his rental car. "This is the nuttiest town on the planet, isn't it, D.C?"

"I don't know. I lived in New York City. I think it's a tie."

168

"No, it's different out here," Pete declared. "Lots of nuts. I saw a guy on the sidewalk before the photo shoot. He was yelling into the sky asking aliens to take him to outer space."

"Seriously?"

"Serious! He was wearing a long coat and a red baseball cap. He was screaming, *Take me home! Come and get me!* It reminded me of when I wanted the aliens to come rescue me off my house. I painted, *LAND HERE* on my roof. When I was studying UFOs I wanted desperately to be picked up."

"You should've moved out here to Hollywood. You would have fit in nicely. I'm pretty sure there are lots of people walking up and down Hollywood Boulevard who have been abducted, probed, and then returned to continuing wandering the walk of fame."

"People love alien stories. You should write a show about that," Pete suggested.

Honestly, I never forgot Pete's quick piece of advice, and the first time I got the opportunity to write a comedy show featuring aliens I seized it. Nell Carter guest starred with Carol Burnett on *Carol and Company,* and I had the privilege of writing a half hour episode I entitled *Spudnik.* Carol played a dear old lady who made a tinfoil hat that attracted signals from space using the energy from a potato, which explains the "spud" in *Spudnik.*

As Pete and I were talking, suddenly, a large German Shepherd dog appeared from behind a car and with a threatening gait, he ran toward Pete.

"Grrrrrrrrrrrr," the dog snarled, as he looked Pete in the eyes.

"Whoa, now!" Pete shouted as he took a step back.

The dog snarled as if he were giving Pete a warning before he attacked.

"Hey! Whose dog?" Pete called out.

Pete and I both backed away, but it was clear that that the dog had no interest in me. The animal wanted to continue moving in on Pete.

Suddenly, a man darted out of a nearby car and dashed toward the dog.

"Stop! Come here, boy!"

The dog froze in place, still staring at Pete and still showing his teeth.

"Get back here!" the owner grumbled as he angrily grabbed the dog's collar and forced him back into his car.

There was no apology. Nothing. The guy started his car and drove away.

Pete was shaken by the moment, but he tried not to show it. For a second, we both thought Pete would be severely attacked by the angry animal.

"This is the craziest town I've ever been in … and I lived in New Orleans!"

"I thought he was going to have you for lunch."

"I'm not going to lie. I thought that, too," Pete replied shaking his head.

"You okay?"

"Yes, but why didn't that dog want you? You're smaller and probably taste better."

"Probably those Richard Petty sunglasses you have on freaked him out. You need to go change your shorts?"

"Funny. Let's go eat."

"Where are you thinking? You're not feeding me tofu or something weird, are you?"

170

"As a matter of fact, there's a place we can walk to I saw earlier."

We walked out of the alley toward the small health food restaurant.

"I can't believe that dog did that," Pete continued.

"Like a scene out of *The Exorcist*," I replied.

"Yes! That's what it felt like."

"You think the Devil is sending you a message?"

"Probably. This town is nuts."

Pete and I walked into the health food restaurant that looked as if it had once been a burger place back in the 1960s. It had large front windows and an A-framed roof. The building was painted a drab green color with yellow accents around the windows and roofline.

We entered the establishment, found a booth, and I stared at the menu as if we were sitting in a foreign country. I was the guy who didn't know the language. Pam joined us for lunch and she and I had the unforgettable privilege of eating our first veggie burger. Pete insisted.

Honestly, I still have the sense memory today, and I hold the same opinion of the burger as I did then. Being raised in one of the largest beef-producing regions in the United States, I have difficulty calling anything but delicious ground beef a "burger."

Pete would be glad to know that since that experience, my family and I are all healthy eaters. We buy and grow as much all-natural foods as possible. We have Pete to thank for helping us re-think our health and what we are putting in our bodies. I think Pete would approve of the changes we've made. And he would be pleased to open the cupboard in our kitchen and find no containers of shortening for Pam's chocolate chip cookies.

171

CHAPTER 17
The Pistol Movie Script Sessions

Questioning Pete Maravich about what events in his life he would prefer to see in his film resulted in some of the most entertaining conversations of our relationship. Pete was usually laid back off the court, but in person he would slip out of the his cool persona and turn into an animated storyteller, full of life, humor, and colorful description.

One of the cassette tapes I found recently contained a story session as we discussed the motion picture project. The book, *Heir to a Dream,* had already gone to print, and Frank wisely pushed us to develop the story and ultimately my writing the screenplay. In retrospect, if we hadn't taken the time to sit with Pete and listen to his wishes, we would have missed out on some important stories as well as precious quality time with the sports legend.

In the beginning of our development of a film based on his life, we considered doing a movie that would span from Pete's childhood to his retirement. When Pete got word that he was to be inducted into the Naismith Memorial Basketball Hall of Fame, it made us reconsider our film's ending. We discussed for a while expanding the story and ending the movie after his induction ceremony.

The following exchanges are based on our conversations about the film, *The Pistol*. Although there was a great deal of discussion about Pete's childhood we hadn't settled on creating a movie based simply on his eighth grade experiences. So, Pete, Frank and I met in my apartment to brainstorm ideas and determine the scope of the film.

My initial thought was to write a film that started in Pete's childhood and ended after he entered the pros as college basketball's greatest scorer and NBA's first million-dollar rookie. I figured his fans would want to witness him breaking Oscar Robertson's all-time scoring record in college and then enjoy seeing Pete entering the professional ranks, but there was always hesitancy. I didn't want us to bite off more than we could chew as first-time filmmakers.

"Whatever part of my life story we tell, I want the movie to have heart. That's the main thing," Pete demanded. "I want people to walk out of the theater and be inspired, no matter what age they are."

As Pete continued telling stories about his adult life and his days in the NBA, the scope of our film grew into a multi-million-dollar motion picture that was way beyond our reach. The stories of Press as a pilot in WWII were amazing and would put viewers on the edge of their seats if written and filmed properly, but that type of film would have a much better chance under the control of a Hollywood studio. It would be millions of dollars that we didn't have. It was our goal to shoot an independent film so we could shepherd the content and tell the story that Pete wanted told.

The following transcript represents Pete's musings regarding what he wanted the film to encompass:

"Yes, there was some conflict in my home, but that came later. My mom was the perfect housewife. I mean that. She never complained about anything. Dad was always out of the house coaching and trying to keep money coming in. I guess we could show Mom getting upset that Dad was never around. You know, the family unit really hasn't changed all that much."

173

"A lot of people can relate to that family dynamic," I chimed in.

" Right. People need something on the screen that they can relate to. I don't care if it was forty years ago, (Pete was thirty-nine at the time of this interview). If I can relate a film to what I'm going through today, it's going to be more interesting to the audience."

"Were you thinking of the pros even when you were a kid in junior high school?"

"Yes! Faith is something that we hope for. I hoped. At that young age I had already seen myself playing twenty years down the road. How? Daydreaming. We can have a scene of me day dreaming about being in the pros. But, you also have to have another scene of me, by myself. I'm sitting there crying and thinking about where I am."

"What do you mean, 'crying?' Why were you upset?" I questioned.

"I'm sitting there thinking that, *What if it never happens? Maybe this dream will never happen. Why do I keep bangin' my head?"*

"So, you had some doubt?"

Pete shook his head and replied, "Honestly, I guess not. There was never a doubt that I would make it. Know why? I had an incredible desire that would never go away. I didn't want to let down my dad and mom and my family and friends. See, in Clemson, they all thought I would be great. I was getting most valuable player awards and hustle awards and it was building my confidence. Deep inside, I didn't want to end up struggling like my dad. You could have a scene like when my dad told me, *Pete, I don't have the money to put you though school. Figure out what you're going to do in the future.* Most kids at that age don't care.'"

174

"It does sound pretty wild that at age twelve you had your mind set on being a pro. Do you think that it will be believable to our audience?" I asked.

"It's what happened. I lived with this great teacher who had come out of nowhere. My dad had done it. I listened to him. When the crowds saw me making shots from twenty-five feet and consistently putting the ball through the hoop from where NBA shooters did, I heard their response from the stands. I wanted to do it again and again."

"What did that feel like; to hear the crowd loving what you were doing?" I asked.

"What did it feel like?" Pete repeated the question as he pondered. "Remember when you got your drivers license, and you took off driving by yourself? It was a thrill. Exciting. I was nervous, but after two blocks my excitement grew stronger. That's how I felt every time I stepped on the court. There was something inside me that kept me seeking that sensation. I kept things inside me during school, but on the court I could get that feeling. I also had a concern for the person sitting in the stands. I wanted them to be entertained so I would come down and make an amazing pass."

"Was it the crowd's reaction that made you happy?"

"Honestly, I wish I could have been more like the people in the stands—more like the fans. The crowd generated my emotions. After the cheers, I was back to wishing for more."

"Was that all you thought about?"

"Yes. I never thought about my opponent."

"Never?" I prodded.

"I didn't care. I just cared about winning. Winning was the most important thing—even more than the fans liking me. It's true. If I didn't shoot, they booed me."

"If you played a game but didn't feel like you played up to your ability, how did that make you feel?"

"If I played a lousy game, even if we won I felt bad. When I was thirteen, I would cover up how I felt. I was aloof. Or, later, like when I was a freshman at LSU, we lost that last game to Kentucky and I walked three miles back to my hotel by myself. I sat in the corner of my hotel room contemplating my life. Two in the morning, my dad came pounding on my hotel room door. 'Pete! Pete, you in there?' I felt like I had let down the world. Seventeen wins and one loss wasn't good enough. All I could think about was the one loss."

"Do you remember where your sense of competition started?"

"Way back. I hated to lose. Ronnie and I would even race each other drinking a glass of milk! My dad would play me one-on-one in the driveway and never let me win. Dad knew my ability. He knew me best."

"What was it like going back to see your old high school?

"It was cool. You know, I had a new coach every year of my high school career. I went to the gym where I played. I walked in there two years ago. That old gym still has tile floors."

"Tile?"

"Yes. Like square tiles."

"What did you do after your games?"

"After games, the kids would go out to get a hamburger at a place called Hoppers Burgers and Fries. I would go there, but I always felt awkward. Mom would come in and find me. She'd say, 'Are you ready, Pete?'"

"Let's put that in the film for sure," I added.

176

"I would leave with my mom, and all my teammates would stay there and have fun. It was okay. All I ever thought about was playing basketball and winning a championship."

"You must have won some championships at some level."

"Not the level I wanted. If I hadn't walked out on the Boston Celtics, I would have had an NBA championship ring."

"They won the championship that year?"

"Yes. In a pre-season game, I scored thirty-eight points and then I walked away from it all. I had battled back from my knee injury, and I played the 1979-1980 season. We didn't play well in the playoffs; just missing the finals. I watched the other guys playing, and I got a sinking feeling. Larry Bird was the young sharpshooter on the team and even though I played, I just didn't feel like I had a future there for the next year."

"Red Auerbach brought you to Boston?"

"Yes. He was a good man, and he respected my skills. He always liked what I did, and he knew I could still play. Good guy. We even did a few TV appearances together. I know I would have played some quality minutes for him, but he wasn't the coach, and the new coach made it pretty clear that he had other guys in mind to play ahead of me. I felt like it was going to be really hard watching a lot of guys playing instead of me. I mean, I was always the guy a team counted on for scoring and assists."

"Describe how it happened? What did you say when you quit?"

"I don't want to say anything bad about anyone."

"I understand," I assured him.

"There was an incident in practice."

"What kind of 'incident?'" I asked.

"Coach had a reputation for working his teams pretty hard, and he wasn't afraid of getting in our faces and screaming what he wanted."

"He would scream at you?" I asked in disbelief.

I admittedly had Pete and other professional basketball players in such a lofty position in my mind that the thought of a coach yelling at my hero and future Hall of Famer surprised me.

"Yes. Pre-season was tough like it always is," Pete continued. "I had been lifting weights and running in the off-season so I could come in and win that championship ring I'd always wanted. You know, I always said that I didn't want to play ten years and retire at thirty, but that's exactly what I did. One of the other players got angry, and he kicked a ball up into the stands. Coach turned to me like I had done it, but it was another player. He went off on me like he was trying to make an example of me."

"That's terrible. What did you say?" I prodded.

"I said something like, *I don't need this*, and then I walked off the floor after practice. I went to the locker room and took off my uniform for the last time. I knew I was done. That was it. That's how my whole life has been. I make quick decisions and move on."

"The Celtics went on to win the championship that year. That had to hurt."

"Oh, I felt fantastic!" Pete laughed and shook his head.

"Sorry. What about your dad? How did he react to that? You were knocking on the door of your life-long dream. His too."

"Oh, man. He was upset. Dad thought I could play forever and keep impacting the game."

I believe a lot of fans would have agreed.

178

"With Pops it's always been about setting high standards and achieving excellence through fundamentals. He wished that I would have played a few more years, but what happened, happened, ya know?

"So, how did you move on with your life?"

"Like I do now. I try to keep my mind on other things to keep me from thinking about what might have been. I want my boys to memorize scriptures. It's like when I used to practice shooting. I used to tell the kids in basketball clinics, *If I read a book a thousand times and you read the same book a hundred times, which one of us is going to know the book better?* When I was awake, that's all I wanted to do was play basketball. It could be raining and storming outside, and I would go out and play in the storm—sometimes at night. I figured if I could dribble in rain and mud in our driveway, I could dribble on any dry hardwood court."

"What did your mom think about you always playing basketball?"

"'She knew it's what made me happy. She knew it made my dad happy. Mom was the best. She was like the mom on *Leave it to Beaver*."

"June Cleaver?"

"Yes! She was just like that. June Cleaver. Her hair was always fixed perfectly, and she wore a dress and an apron when she was cooking. She was June. I was the Beaver! Hah! She did get worried like if it was lightning when I was out there in the driveway, but for me, that made it even better. We're putting that in the movie. That would be cool with the lightning and everything. How do you guys do that?" Pete wondered.

"We'll use a rain machine and the lighting guys will make it look like lightning," I assured him.

179

"It's all pretending for you Hollywood guys, isn't it?"

"Well, yes and no. We pretend, but we really have to work at it."

"Work at pretending?"

"Hey, you worked at playing a game," I poked back defending my industry.

"Good point," Pete agreed.

"Yeah. It's a living," I laughed.

"Right," Pete laughed, skeptically at me, "Like *Days of Our Lives*?"

"Seven days a week; sometimes ten or twelve hour days. Or more. People have no idea the hours the soap opera writers work. It's a bit insane at times."

"Hollywood is a trip. I don't know how you live here. Do you and Pam like it?"

"We do. We love it. We've made a lot of friends. Our friends in Los Angles are like family and always will be."

"And you're going to have kids?"

"Got one on the way."

"Okay, this story is for the book, not the movie," Pete explained before continuing his thoughts. Remember the bedroom in my house?"

Pete was referring to the master bedroom. The bed was the first super king size bed I had ever seen.

"About seven people your size could fit in that bed, Darrel," Pete teased. "The Seven Dwarfs."

"Yeah, yeah, I get it. You know, I'm 5' 8', not 4' 8'."

"In that room is where I got saved. I was retired, and I was really frustrated. All I had known was basketball. Suddenly, I didn't know what to do with myself with all that time on my hands. But it was worse than that. I didn't feel like my life had any purpose anymore. I was ready to end it all."

180

"You really wanted to die?"

"Yes. It was the night I told you about when I was I was driving my Porsche across Lake Pontchartrain Bridge. I was going about a hundred and thirty or so, and I said to myself, *Just turn the wheel right now and smash into the bridge rails. You'll die instantly, and that will end all the torment!* You know, I had been into Eastern mystical religions and ufology. One night I got up on the roof with a flashlight, and I tried to get aliens to abduct me. I'm serious!"

I'm sure I looked at Pete as if he had lost his mind, but I was actually trying to picture Pete on a roof shouting to aliens.

"I don't know how I didn't turn the wheel and end it all, but I obviously didn't. I kept driving and parked the car next to the house. I climbed into bed with my wife, and she was sleeping."

"Did you fall asleep?" I asked.

"No way. After a while, my entire body was covered in sweat. I was soaked. My heart was racing, and I could tell something had to change in my life or it was going to be over. I got out of bed, and got on my knees, and for the first time in a long time I said a prayer for God to be real in my life. I said, *God, if you're real, show me.* And Darrel, I know you're going to think I'm crazy, but I heard an audible voice."

"God talked out loud to you?"

"He talked to me in an audible voice. You know, you hear people say they heard God's voice? I'm telling you, man, I heard His voice. Not like inside my mind; I'm talking about I really heard it! He said, *Be strong. Lift thine own heart.*"

"You heard that?" I questioned.

"I literally heard that. Man, it filled the whole room and I knew it must have woke up my wife. I got off my knees and shook her awake and I really scared her. I said, *Did you hear that?* But she hadn't heard a thing. She probably thought I was crazy. I told her, *God just spoke to me! Out loud!* And just like that, the horrible feeling I had a few minutes before was gone. I mean, when you hear the voice of God, it changes everything. It might not happen to many people, but that's how it happened to me, and I knew without a doubt that God was and is real."

Pete's passionate explanation of the most profound moment in his life was exhilarating to me. This was the Pete Maravich that my friend had told me about. This was a man who had been radically changed from his days of playing basketball. The same zeal he had as a young player was what I was hearing as he explained why he was a different person now. The fact that his conversion came on the heels of his near-suicide experience put things in perspective for me. It was like coming to the end of the game clock and the time was running out. Pete had to sink the winning shot or suffer the ultimate game-ending defeat.

"I have never been the same, Darrel. I want all that in the book. Don't sugarcoat it. I'm going to tell everybody what happened and how it happened; even the audible voice I heard. I know folks will think I'm nuts, but it's what happened and the truth is the truth. You guys hungry?"

"A burger would be great."

Pete shook his head indicating his disappointment in my suggestion.

"You've never tried the burgers at Hamptons in Toluca Lake, Pete."

"Is that where you Hollywood stars hang out?" he poked at me again.

"Yes. We all hang out there." I joked. "There's one on Riverside Boulevard in Toluca Lake, and the original one is on Highland in Hollywood. It has a huge tree growing out of the middle of the building. I've never had a bad hamburger there. Cooked to order, and then you pile on it whatever you like at the salad bar. I'll take you there when you come to Los Angeles. They have a slam dunk burger you should try."

"When I was a kid back in Clemson, there was a soda shop we'd go to if we had a dime or quarter. They had burgers and fries. It was like back in the day with the soda jerk and the counter. You could get Dr. Pepper floats and stuff like that."

"There was a place like that in my hometown called McShane's," I chimed in. "They made root beer floats."

"That soda shop is where I bet a kid that I could spin a basketball on my finger for an hour. I bet him so he would pay for my ice cream float."

"Did you spin it for an hour?"

Pete demonstrated how he did it. He picked up a basketball and began spinning it. I had watched him spin a basketball on TV, but there was something different about watching him spin it inches from my face.

"The secret is that I didn't just spin it on one finger. I used several fingers," Pete smiled as he kept spinning it. "This is called fanning the ball."

As the ball spun on his index finger at a blurring speed, with his other hand, Pete grazed the ball using a slapping motion to keep it spinning like a top. Suddenly, he switched fingers from the index to his middle finger, and then his ring finger, his thumb and then to his index finger.

183

"The kid didn't count on me switching fingers. I didn't count on my index finger breaking a nail and bleeding, but when I thought of switching fingers it just came naturally to me. So, an hour later I got a free soda."

"And you impressed all the kids watching."

"Yeah, it was like the Pied Piper story. The longer I kept spinning the ball, the more kids would gather around to watch. One hour later, I stopped and everybody cheered like I was Rocky Balboa or something."

"That's definitely in the book and in the movie," I assured him.

"Yeah, do the old time-lapse and fade in and out thing because it really was an hour. You guys will know how to do that in the movie. Right?"

"It'll be a great scene, Pete. Definitely."

"I did all kinds of crazy things like that. Wherever I went I had a basketball in my hand. I took it to school. I slept with it like a Teddy bear. I took it into the movie theater with me and dribbled on the aisle during the movie. Of course, it was like during a matinee when it was just me in there watching the film, but I really did it."

"I heard you dribbled out the car window when your dad was driving."

"It's true. Dad was coaching at the college and I would go straight from school to the college so I could work out with the Clemson University team."

"You worked out with the college guys?" I asked skeptically.

"Sure. My dad would put me in the drills, and I would show the guys new ball-handling drills Dad had taught me."

"Was he motivating you or his players?" I asked.

184

"I guess he figured a little eighth grader scrimmaging with college guys would push them, and at the same time make me better."

"Dad would say, *You have to conceptualize the game when you play. Your mind has to be two or three steps ahead of everyone else; thinking about what could happen as you are bringing the ball down the court.*"

"Do you think it made you better?"

"I know it did. Look, if I could dribble and shoot against guys a foot taller than me and bigger than me, then I figured I could take on any junior high kid my age. You know I made my high school team when I was in the eighth grade."

"At Daniel?"

"Yes. That should be in the movie, too. I mean, there I was, a foot shorter than my brother and I was playing right along with him."

"Wait. Your brother was what grade?"

"He was a senior."

"Tell me more about him."

"Honestly, the main thing I can tell you is that he was a better basketball player than I was."

"Pete. Come on," I replied incredulously.

"Seriously. He was an outstanding player. Dad had taught him a lot too, but I gotta say, he was more naturally gifted than me. He was fast and tall and he could shoot from anywhere."

"How did he handle the fact that his little brother would be playing on the team?"

"Well, he dealt with it. He was the star player and leading scorer. I'm telling you, he was really a good player."

It was the first time I had given any thought to what kind of impact the big brother of the family would have had on Pete. I had always heard about the wiz kid basketball phenom who was coached by his dad. They even featured that fun fact on the back of Pete's professional basketball cards. I had to know more about his brother, if Pete would tell me.

"Yes, I can tell you about him."

Until that moment, I hadn't thought of Ronnie as a pivotal or important part of Pete's story, but as I thought about my childhood and how much my two older brothers impacted my life, I felt there could be some valuable information waiting for me.

"Ronnie played half a year at Georgia Southern, and then he quit to serve in the military. He thought it would be cool to sign up and go over to Vietnam. I think they glamorized the whole thing back then, and for some of the guys enlisting in military service was a way to gain acceptance."

"How good was Ronnie as a player?"

"He was always the shooting and rebound leader. He was better than me, for sure."

"Serious?"

"I'm serious. Ronnie was really good."

"What did he think about you and how you made it to all the way to the NBA?"

"No way my brother thought I would go that far. He knew I had skills, but I was the little brother. He thought I would make it to college and play ball, but not turn pro."

"What would be Ronnie's memories of you as a little brother ... as a kid?"

"Just me playing basketball constantly."

"I see."

"It's all I thought about, and that was my childhood. Ronnie used to say it was strange when girls would come up to him and ask about me. He had lots of girls after him, but when I got older and made it to the pros I guess they talked to him to get to me." Pete laughed.

I couldn't help but think that there must have been a vast difference if one compared Press and Pete's relationship with Press and Ronnie's relationship.

"When I asked Ronnie about Dad, he said, 'I'm going to miss Dad when he's gone.'"

It was a reminder of how people can grow up in the same house with the same parents, yet their lives can have such different outcomes. I couldn't help but wonder what it would have been like had Ronnie pursued basketball in college. Better yet, what would it have looked like if Pete and his big brother had played together while being coached by their father at LSU?

When Pete told me that his brother was a better player than he was, it made me ponder what might have been had they played together at a collegiate level. Imagine a taller, faster and stronger big brother playing with Pistol Pete Maravich. I'll leave that to your imagination and mine.

CHAPTER 18
Heir to the Dreamer

"When a father gives to his son, both laugh; when a son gives to his father, both cry."
- William Shakespeare

September of 1986, I got a copy of a letter that Pete longed for me to see. The top of the letterhead was imprinted with a logo and the words under it read *Naismith Memorial Basketball Hall of Fame* in bold letters.

"Dear Pete: Congratulations on your nomination for election to the Naismith Memorial Hall of Fame. Your file has been processed by the Screening Committee and forwarded to the Honors Committee for final consideration.

The Executive Committee and the Board of Trustees have voted unanimously to adopt a revised process for nomination and election to the Hall of Fame.

The major thrust of this plan is to open up the selection phases to the public.

The first significant change involved the publishing of the names of the Screening Committee chaired by Bob Cousy. The second important change introduces the publication of the names of the individuals who have proceeded through the Screening Committee and are eligible for election.

It is our hope that you will understand the importance of this revised policy. If we do not hear from you to the contrary prior to September 30, we will release your name along with the other nominees to the national media.

You, your family, and friends should take justifiable pride that you are being considered for this coveted honor. Good luck!

"So, you're in? Congratulations!" I congratulated Pete. "You'll be the youngest player ever inducted into the Hall of fame?"

"I think so," Pete smiled as he tried his best to maintain humble.

"This means that the letter you read in front of your classroom when you were thirteen years old has come true. All of it."

"Not quite. It's not a championship ring," Pete replied.

"Your report you read in class stated that you wanted to grow up to become a professional basketball player, you wanted to get paid to play basketball, you wanted to be the first basketball player to sign a million dollar contract, and you wanted to win a big ring that proved you were one of the best."

"Yes, but I meant I wanted to win a championship and get a championship ring."

"Pete, lots of players have played in the NBA championship game, but many of the guys who played in that game never won it. Only a fraction of guys who played professionally are inducted into the Hall of Fame. The ring you will receive and the bust of you that they will put in the Hall signifies that you were one of the best professional basketball players ever; one of the best of all time. I say your dreams all came true."

"You gonna put that in the movie?"

"It's already in ... I mean, the part where you read the letter."

189

Legendary people are called legends for a reason. They accomplish extraordinary things, and stories about their undertakings often live forever. Unfortunately, the good news about the Hall of Fame selection was dampened by the health battle Press was fighting. It was heartbreaking to know that as I wrote exciting stories about how courageous Press was, he was lying in a bed in Pete's house in Louisiana, and I would probably never see him again. The unexpected letter I had received from Press was becoming more valuable each day.

When Pete and I began his autobiography we spent hours talking about how close his father and he had been throughout Pete's lifetime. From the first hours in Pete's cradle until the end of his father's life they were best friends. The bond between the two men was never closer than the last few weeks when Pete set out to save his father's life.

Doctors had done everything in their power to prolong Press's days, but in December of 1986, after a speaking engagement in Florida, Pete witnessed first-hand just how bad things had become for his father. For the first time he allowed himself to ponder the reality of Press dying. They had attended a basketball game and on their drive back home Press climbed into the back of the car, curled up in the seat and slept from Orlando to Clearwater. Press was in bad shape according to Pete. Instead of going to Louisiana to spend Christmas with Pete's family, Press wound up in a hospital emergency room where he was diagnosed with pneumonia.

Because Pete wanted Press near him as much as possible, Pete prepared the guest room. It's the room where Press encouraged Frank to set the price on the *Homework Basketball* videos low so every kid in America could afford them. Press was extremely ill, but his heart was always for others, especially kids wanting to improve their game.

190

"I couldn't stand hearing him cough so hard," Pete explained. "Dad kept coughing and coughing and the doctors prescribed him ten different medicines. When he would cough, I wondered if the cancer had gotten into his lungs. I'll never forget my dad telling me one night that he wished he had done something else with his life, like become a doctor so he could've helped people."

I thought of the thousands of young people who were impacted by the coaching of Press Maravich. His influence as an instructor and innovator of the game stretched around the globe. The number of motivated and inspired players who attended hundreds of *Homework Basketball* sessions is truly incalculable. What the youngsters learned from Press, they surely passed that knowledge on to their sons and daughters who played the game. The dozens of Press Maravich shooting, ball-handling, dribbling and passing drills that he invented are still being perfected today thanks to *Homework Basketball* DVD's.

"I wish I could've helped people," Press said remorsefully as he coughed.

"I told Pop to stop talking like that because his influence will be felt around the world for generations. I reminded him that all the games he had coached are memories in someone's life. I went on to tell him how much he is respected and how much he is still admired by people he will never meet."

Eventually, the cancer had reached a point where the once-strong basketball player and coach could only lie in silence in his bed. Finally, he began refusing food and liquids and his immune system was depleted.

"I've prayed like I had never prayed before," Pete informed me over the telephone.

"So, there's nothing else you can do?"

"I'm going to Germany to see if they can help Pop. There's a specialist over there that is trying new things that they aren't doing here in the U.S. I'm never going to give up. I can't. He would never give up on me, and I won't give up on him."

"Pam and I are praying for you, Pete. As soon as you know something, please give us a call."

When Pete and Press boarded the airplane destined for Hanover, Germany, Pete was fully aware that the trip itself could spell the end of Press. After landing safely in Germany, Pete said the next two weeks spent in the hospital with his dad were two of the most important weeks of his life.

"Don't get your hopes too high, Mister Maravich," the doctor told Pete in a thick German accent.

"Do what it takes. He's tougher than he looks," Pete told him.

The doctor warned Pete not to think that he was some sort of miracle worker. Press's body was under attack from the cancer and the pneumonia had weakened Press to a dangerous level. He was at death's door. Surprisingly, within hours the medical treatment cleared the hacking cough that Press had dealt with for the last five months. It was hard not to get hopes up after seeing such a sudden and positive sign.

"Pop's cough went away, and as the protocol started for the cancer I could physically see him changing and re-sponding positively to it. I just kept praying that it was the be-ginning of his healing, and that we could go back home to re-sume our normal lives."

"Describe for me what you did while Press was being treated. I mean, how did you spend those long days?"

"I had my Bible, and I committed myself to being an encouragement to him. I found all the verses I could about believing and healing. I had a routine I followed each day. I arrived at the hospital and sat next to Pop's bed. I would read the Bible to him and I would pray. I did that day and night. One evening, as I returned to my room, I was so exhausted from praying for Dad's healing that I just fell to my knees and I cried. I cried and I begged God. *Please, please, God. Please heal Dad. I am helpless without you. I am nothing without you.* I just kept crying," Pete said in a somber tone.

"When did you know your efforts weren't working?"

"When the doctors sent us home with lots of drugs that he would need every day for the rest of his life," Pete said as he shook his head. "The cancer had spread too far. It was in his lungs and there was nothing they could do. A new friend I had made in Germany came to the hospital to give Pop and me a ride to the airport. It had been almost four decades since my dad had carried me out of the hospital with hopes and dreams of my future and our future together. As I picked up my dad in my arms and carried him down the hall of the hospital, it washed over me just how drastically the tables had turned."

The flight home was a nightmare for Press and Pete. Back when airlines had smoking sections, Pete discovered that the only seats available were in one of those smoking sections near the tail of the aircraft and breathing was already difficult for Press.

"There wasn't anything I could do. I raised the armrest between our seats and I made Dad as comfortable as I could. I covered him with a blanket, and I stood in the back of the airplane for most of the ten-hour flight. All I could do was pray."

"I'm sure you couldn't take your eyes off of him."

"Right. It seemed like all day and through the night I was giving Dad a shot or a pill. Someone told me that there is no pain that compares to bone cancer pain. It got so bad for Dad that we had to give him morphine, but that made him sick. It was obvious that he was running out of time."

Pete grew weary of recounting the moments of trying to save his father. I was witnessing a change. From the death of Press until the last day I was with Pete, my friend was changing. There was serious countenance on his face that I had never seen. Our discussions weren't so light and full of humor as they had been in the years and months before.

I asked Pete to compose a few paragraphs regarding the Germany trip and try to help me understand what was going on in his heart and mind during the sad and regrettable trip. The point that Pete wanted to get across to the reader of *Heir to a Dream* was his true feelings for his father.

In late March of 1987, Press was so sick that Pete had to have him admitted into a hospital in Louisiana. Pete cancelled all of his commitments, including speaking engagements he had scheduled around the country. He was resolved to stay by his father's side until Press either miraculously received a healing or God took him home. So many people had given up on Press in the past, but Pete remained consistent.

"I reminded Dad that God had never called on anyone to give up," Pete said.

The time spent in the Louisiana hospital became a time of spiritual growth for Pete. He thought he was there to pour into his father all the biblical wisdom he could in order for his Dad to believe and experience a miraculous healing. Pete later realized that there was much more to learn from the man who had taught him so much during their lives together.

"People don't understand the close relationship I had with my Dad. People would say I was his puppet or robot. No. My dad was the best dad a kid could ever have. Every good memory I have of my father includes his eyes and his words. When he talked to me, he looked me in the eyes. When he taught me things, I hung on every word. His emotions were often transferred to me. When my Dad laughed, that made me happy. When he was struggling with my Mom or disappointments with his coaching jobs, I felt bad for him. I was somehow tied to his passions. That's how close we were."

In short, Pete told me that whatever happened to his dad happened to him. His father's sadness was his sadness. His happiness was always connected to Pete's happiness. When Press was fired from LSU, Pete felt rejected as well.

Finally, when Press was tormented with the pain of cancer, Pete said he felt the agony of it too. It was apparent that more than blood and DNA connected the heir to the original dreamer. There was a spiritual connection that was inexplicable.

"My relationship with Pop was unique. Because of all those years of being so close, and after all his giving to me, I wanted to give all I was to him until he breathed his last breath," Pete said.

During the final days of Press's life, Pete miraculously saw his father full of joy despite the excruciating pain he was enduring. There was one more lesson being taught to Pete through the sickness and death of his dad.

"Dad felt only love. In his heart, the true manifestation of a miracle was his complete forgiveness for others."

As Pete sat by Press's hospital bed he held his father's hand and prayed for hours upon end.

195

Pete said that he learned from Press that it's one thing to talk about the battle and another to actually fight the battle. Bitterness was never allowed to enter the battle for Press. When he nearly stopped breathing a few times, Press never gave up the fight. Because Press was giving his all to live, Pete dedicated himself to serving in anyway he could. He spent forty-eight hour shifts by his father's near-lifeless body. Pete watched his father breath and he watched the minutes click by on the wall clock. Often, Pete noticed Press praying through the pain.

One night, Press opened his eyes and looked at Pete as best he could. Taking Pete by the hand, Press whispered, *You remind me of myself years ago. My dad died in my arms and it gives me comfort to know that I will die in yours.*

The final words that Pete told his father was that he would never give up. *I promise I'll stand by this bed until you breathe your last breath. When that last breath happens, I will give in and stop believing for the healing miracle.*

Pete's hope for his father's complete and miraculous healing never wavered. He even imagined the future when he would stand on a stage with his dad during speaking engagements.

"Someday, I'll be with you, Pop," Pete whispered in Press's ear.

Those were the last words Press Maravich heard before his breathing completely stopped and his heart faded into its last beat. Pete watched as his father passed away and the heart monitor by the bed flat lined. On April 15, 1987, Press and Pete were separated in this life for the first time. That may seem like an interesting way to describe it, but that's the way Pete did.

"Darrel, I kept talking to Dad. I really believe that for a few minutes after his heart stopped he could still hear me. You hear about people who have near-death experiences hovering over their dead body when they pass away? I believe that. I told Pop that I would see him soon, and that I was so happy for him because he was with Jesus," Pete told me with the conviction of a pastor preaching a sermon.

"When I get to Heaven, Pop will turn around and look at me as if I have been there all along," Pete smiled.

"What do you mean?"

"Think about it. There's no time in Heaven. It'll be just like Pop just got there and then I'll be there. And then we will spend eternity together. That should make anyone excited to think about!"

Pete was a guest speaker at a Billy Graham revival, two weeks after Press died. He mesmerized the thousands in attendance as he told the story of his father and how he and his dad looked for happiness everywhere and in everything but where they could truly find it. Pete repeated his now famous line about when he found Jesus, happiness found him. Most of all, Pete was impressed by how Press had taught him about faith.

The passing of such a great man saddened us all. Although I had only known him a couple of years, Press made a life-long impression on me. His letters and his words of encouragement to me will never be forgotten. As I mentioned in the beginning of this book, Press reminded me so much of my father. They had so much in common, and yet they lived very different lives. When I heard Press's voice on the other end of a telephone call he sounded like my dad. When I sat with him in his apartment I felt like my dad should have been sitting there with us telling his war stories as well.

197

Press and my father were children during the Great Depression in America. They had both suffered tragic losses of family members. Both were U.S. Army veterans who miraculously survived near-death experiences during WWII. Press died on April 15th. You can imagine what was racing through my mind when my father also died on April 15th.

Peter Press Maravich, the original dreamer of this story, died at age seventy-one at Highland Park Hospital in Covington, Louisiana. His funeral service was held at the Wildwood Chapel in Aliquippa, Pennsylvania, his childhood home. His body was laid to rest in the Saint Elijah Serbian Orthodox Church Cemetery.

Pam and I couldn't make arrangements to get to Aliquippa, but a few days later I received a small padded envelope that helped ease my disappointment. Inside the envelope was a cassette tape that featured Pete giving the eulogy for his father.

When I began this book, I developed a habit of reaching a certain point in my writing and then returning to my large filing cabinet full of Pistol Pete Maravich papers and memories. When I reached this part of the story I got excited when I remembered the tape I had received in April of 1987. Since obtaining the tape, Pam and I moved to two different homes in Los Angeles and four different residences in Missouri. Honestly, I hadn't listened to the tape since I opened the envelope over thirty years ago.

I'm happy to report that the lost cassette tape was found in a blue plastic box tucked away in our attic. What you are about to read is a sampling of what I was able to transpose. Full disclosure—the tape broke off the reel twice and I had to take it apart and glue the tape to both reels before I could listen to it. It was well worth the effort.

Press Maravich's funeral was held April 18, 1987 in Aliquippa, Pennsylvania, the town he had great respect for, but the city he wished to escape so desperately. Reverend Nick Radovich at the Wildwood Chapel conducted the memorial service.

A few notables in Press's life spoke as Pete and the family looked on. Coach John Lotz, best known as Coach Dean Smith's assistant at North Carolina as well as head coach at Florida, read scriptures from 1 Thessalonians and 1 Corinthians. Coach Lotz's friendship and spiritual guidance was instrumental in Pete's maturity as a new Christian. The service featured a few traditional hymns such as "I Surrender All" sung in Serbian.

There was a touching moment when Press's stepbrother, Sam Kosanovich, stepped behind the microphone and told the mourners, *We are here because of the resurrection of Jesus Christ. The family and I would like to thank you. I lost a brother a few months ago and now Press. I know they both had a personal relationship with Christ. I know that I will see him someday soon. I thank you, Lord, for the salvation of my brother because I will see him soon.*

Reverend Donnie Lyles, a family friend and Press's pastor from Clearwater shared a few stories about Press. Pastor Lyles started a church in Clearwater and Pete encouraged Lyles to meet Press, a new Christian at that time. The following is a portion of what Reverend Lyles said:

"I met Press four years ago when I spoke at his basketball camp," Lyles recalled. "Press said, *Preacher, you did a good job.* Pete asked me if I would lead a Bible study with just his Dad and him. I said I would. So, I met with them after lunch and I shared scriptures with Press. Press had a lot of questions. A lot of the questions were about forgiveness."

Pastor Lyles continues telling the story of the time Press visited a local church in October of 1985, and during the sermon God started dealing with his thoughts and his heart. Press said he didn't recall everything the preacher was saying, but Press considered the huge change he had witnessed in Pete's life. Press said he wanted to know Jesus the way Pete knew him, but during the pastor's invitation to accept Jesus, no one in the congregation went down the aisle.

When Donnie Lyles moved to Clearwater he and Press got together for lunch. Press informed the pastor that he would gladly be the first member of the new church Lyles was starting, and after a few weeks it was evident that Press was one of the most faithful members. Lyles described the kind of church member Press became. During church services Press would boldly request prayers for his family and friends around the country. At the end of Sunday church services, Press would faithfully drop money into an offering basket on his way out of the church. Although going to church had never been his lifestyle, Press proved himself to be a faithful member. One Monday morning, Donnie got an unexpected call from Press because he had forgotten to drop his offering money into the basket as he left the service. The pastor received the envelope from Press a few days later.

The funeral celebrated the new man that Press had become since his conversion to Christianity. The family and pastors read articles in the newspapers written after Press's death that mentioned the fiery temper for which Press was known. That characterization was very hurtful to the family because they had witnessed his spiritual and personal transformation. Most notably, his fiery temper had disappeared.

Lyles continued the tribute recounting an incident that happened during the last basketball camp in which he had participated. Press caught some of the young campers breaking the camp rules and as far as Press was concerned, the only solution was to send the rule-breakers back to their respective homes as punishment.

Pastor Lyles stepped into the situation and shared with Press a Bible verse about God's mercy. He suggested that Press show the young boys mercy because the Heavenly Father had shown him mercy. Press pondered that option and then went to the campers and extended mercy to them. Those young men will never forget the moment they were extended leniency from a man who a year earlier may not have been so malleable.

Pastor Lyles mentioned that when it came time to pray in church, Press would start to pray but before he could speak he would begin to cry as he thought about all the people in his life that he loved. It was another example of how wrong the sports reporters were about the person of Press Maravich. Gentleness and tenderness were two of the words used often to describe the former coach. Pastor Lyles asked the Maravich family what changes they had seen in him. The list was long and consistently mentioned his gentleness. The list also included the absence of profane language in Press's vocabulary.

Lyles reminded those in attendance that the Bible says, *bitter and sweet water can't flow out of the same heart.* The family also mentioned that Press had a greater love for others. Pastor Donnie Lyles wrapped up his thoughts when he said that Press had learned to cast his cares upon the Lord because He cared for him.

As I listened carefully to the cassette tape, I heard the moment I had been waiting for.

201

I think I had been so busy writing *Heir to a Dream* at the time I received the cassette that I never took time to listen to it. The church was quiet. Pete approached the microphone and apparently his walking to the podium to speak was a surprise to everyone. Here is what he said:

"I wasn't planning on getting up here this morning," Pete began in a very tired and weak sounding voice. "It's very difficult to be here, but I wanted to share with everyone some of the things that happened the last five-and-a-half months. We traveled over 20,000 miles, including northern Germany, where a foremost cancer specialist told me that my dad's cancer was all over his body. Pop fought until his last breath. He suffered for the last three months and was on morphine for the pain."

Pete cleared his throat and continued, "The morphine caused more problems, but he would never cry out. He would just pray. His arms were completely black. They couldn't find veins to give him any more shots."

Pete paused to gather his thoughts.

"I saw people who didn't know who we were. They didn't know "Pistol Pete" or my dad. They would walk out of his room in tears saying they had never seen anyone endure so much without complaining. When the nurse gave him medicine he would shake and he would spill water on the bed sheets. He could hardly swallow."

Emotion gripped Pete. His voice quivered.

"Then, dad would apologize for spilling the water. There was a portable toilet right by the bed. To get out of bed and to take that one step to get to it was like a marathon. It would take him twenty minutes to get there and back."

The church was completely silent as Pete paused. He took a deep breath to continue as best he could.

202

"From nine o'clock in the morning to nine o'clock at night we would stay in the scriptures. I would walk to my room. It was cold, and I would walk in the snow and get in to my room and tell God how helpless we were and that our only hope was in Him. As a child, my dad took me everywhere. Whenever he went somewhere, I went with him. He did that for me, and in the end it put us on a higher realm—a higher spiritual plateau. Our relationship was so close. We used to argue, but we had a closeness that people didn't understand. I thought God was using me to teach him. But he was teaching me."

At that moment, Pete's voice cracked and he cried. A few seconds later he composed himself and continued, "It's one thing to talk about battle, but it is another thing to do battle. For three years he never wavered. My dad was bitter for years and years. I used to hate everyone who stabbed us in the back and did things they shouldn't have done. In the end, my dad didn't have one ounce of bitterness. My dad said to me, *It seems like yesterday that I was where you are. I was with my stepfather when he died in my arms. It comforts me that you are here.*"

Pete must have looked around the room at that moment to see Press's stepbrother Sam Kosanovich and other extended family members in the congregation.

"He talked about you ... all of you. He could hardly breathe, but he read your cards and it meant so much that you cared for him. My dad loved you. He loved you more than when you used to know him. And the only thing that I can say is that my only hope is Jesus Christ."

True to form, scripture came to Pete's mind.

Like David after he lost his son, they asked, *Why are you not mourning?* David answered, *My son can't come to me anymore, but one day I will come to him.*"

Pete paused another moment to collect his thoughts.

"Someday, I will be with my dad. We live by faith and not by sight. I will tell you, God loves you. My dad loved you. If you could have seen his last days—for hours he would pray. He was at peace with God. I asked him one hour before he died, and he said that he had no pain. He could have injected morphine for the pain, but he didn't. For three-and-a-half weeks he had no morphine. Minutes before he died I told him that I would continue to believe that he would be healed. I told him that I would believe until his last breath. The last thing I told my father was, *I want you to know that I will be with you soon ... and ... I love you ... and so does everyone else.*"

And that was the end of Pete's words to the mourners on that tremendously sad day. Pete tried to honor and celebrate Press's life, but for Pete it was as if he had lost part of his heart. In my opinion, Pete was never quite the same.

CHAPTER 19
Life Without Press Maravich

"My father gave me the greatest gift anyone could give another person; he believed in me." – Jim Valvano

"My father won't get to witness one of his biggest dreams," Pete murmured. "He wanted to be there for my induction into the Hall of Fame."

A few days after accepting the Hall of Fame honor, Pete told me, "When I accepted the award, the honor made it even more clear just how much of an impact my dad had on my life."

Pete was inducted into the Naismith Memorial Basketball Hall of Fame on May 5, 1987, just twenty days after the death of his father. The emptiness for Pete was nearly overwhelming. As he sat on the podium with great players like Bobby Houbregs, Walt Frazier, Bobby Wanzer, and Rick Barry, all Pete could think of was how Press should have been standing behind the podium giving the acceptance speech for him.

"It was my dad who should have had the Hall of Fame medal hung around his neck."

How fitting it is that the name enshrined in the hall is *Peter Press Maravich*, "Pistol Pete's" given name—his father's name. When Pete read his name on his Hall of Fame statue, all he could think about was Press. The text of Pete's acceptance speech into the Hall of Fame can be found there, so I decided to include in this book something a bit more unique for his fans—a prayer he gave at the Hall of Fame.

After all, this book is meant to be full of stories and tidbits you cannot find in other Pete Maravich biographies. The prayer reveals to all admirers of his life exactly where Pete's heart was shortly before his death at age forty. The prayer went like this:

Heavenly Father, we have gathered here this morning before Thy presence with thanksgiving and praise. We sing in our hearts for joy to You, O Lord, and we that know You shout joyfully because You are the Rock of our salvation. Father, Your word says that "man is like a mere breath; his days like a passing shadow." Make us realize the shortness of our days here upon this earth so that we will begin to utilize the precious time You give to each of us for the winning of souls to the kingdom. Give to us that know You the desire and power to boldly and confidently witness what Christ has done in each of our lives.

Your word also says in Matthew 16:26, "For what will a man be profited if he gains the whole world, and forfeits his soul; or what will a man give in exchange for his soul?" What upon this earth is worth the eternal loss of one's soul? Father, there is no amount of money that one can have, or material things one can possess, nor prestigious awards one can receive, or even power that one can own which will ever fill the void and godly-shaped vacuum that is present within the hearts of all people who have said "no" to the Savior. For all that is external and physical is but for a fleeting, temporary moment, compared to the inexplicable joy when the truth of Jesus Christ comes home into one's heart, and a lasting peace which is permanent and eternal.

My prayer this morning, Father, is for the light of the gospel of Christ to penetrate the darkness here this weekend. Your word says in Psalms 149:10, "The senseless and the stupid shall alike perish." I also pray for an injury-free game and travel mercies to all as they leave for home. I pray for all these things in the magnificent, wonderful name of Jesus. Amen.

That was the heart of Pete Maravich. What would otherwise be a simple prayer, Pete found a way to celebrate and evangelize.

My editor at Thomas Nelson wanted me to include an epilogue to *Heir to a Dream* that would elaborate upon the Hall of Fame induction and the death of Press. A few days later I received three typed pages that Pete wanted me to submit.

Much of his original writing made it into the final pages, but when I pulled the three pages from my filing cabinet for this book, I realized there were a few things I could add. The following words from Pete are from our telephone conversation, as well as his text from his tribute:

My dad talked about the day I would be inducted into the Hall. I told him that my receiving that honor was his dream, not mine. His vision of me on the stage someday accepting the greatest accolade a professional basketball player can achieve was solidly in line with his belief that I could become the greatest player to ever play. That's what drove my dad to teach me, mold me, and encourage me to be a little better every day of my life. Of course, he had the dream of my playing on a world championship team, but his biggest hope for me was to get the praise he thought I deserved and see my name listed among the game's greatest in the Hall of Fame.

207

I told Pop that if they ever called my name in Spring-
field, Massachusetts, I would stop the ceremony and tell them
to give the award to my dad. He deserves it more than I. I keep
thinking of the word "commitment" when I think of my induc-
tion to the Hall of Fame.

Pete wasn't referring to all the thousands of hours he
had committed to becoming a professional player worthy of
the Hall of Fame. He was talking about the commitment his
father had made to Pete's success. Pete continues:

You don't realize things like that until the person is
gone. I never stopped to think of the thousands of hours of his
life that he devoted to seeing me become better than him! Alt-
hough I was watching the death of my father those last few
months of his life, being with him was an experience that I
would wish for any kid and his father. It was during those
tough times that I got to put things straight with my dad. We
talked about everything. I wanted everything on the table be-
fore he left me. I was able to look him in the eyes and ask his
forgiveness for all the times I messed up and hurt him. I got to
be a champion for my dad, but in a way I never had thought.
When we were with the doctors, and as we sought world-class
healthcare I got to step in and be his advocate, his daily sup-
port, and his constant prayer warrior. What a privilege it was
to be by his side in death after all his years of being by my side
in life!

In the last few months of Pete's life, going through the
days and weeks without his father became very difficult. His
emotional pain transitioned into physical pain. His heart ached
without his dad. That was the time I noticed another change in
my hero.

The speeches he gave became more passionate regarding his plea for people to find the same answer for their lives that he had. In a very strange way, it was as if he knew the time clock of his life was in the fourth quarter. Pete didn't share with me any premonition he had regarding his death, but he made very enigmatic remarks during his public speaking, his testimonies, and during his prayer breakfast speeches. During one of his speeches he said almost as a matter of fact, *I don't have much time left.* He clearly meant that he didn't have much time left on Earth. There was also an oft-repeated quote that has been reprinted in hundreds of articles when Pete said in 1974 that he didn't want to play ten years in the pros, retire, and die at age forty. Pete was struck by the reality of the brevity of life when he watched Press die.

Although Pete and I would have more light-hearted times ahead doing a book tour and signings and other public appearances, I detected subtle differences in my friend and business partner. There was the pain of loss, and there was obvious "physical pain" he was experiencing as well. After Press died, I saw Pete physically change. He looked tired. At times, he didn't possess the same energy as when I met him a couple of years earlier. People we met often asked privately if Pete was doing "okay." I would simply tell them that Pete had been through a lot recently. Never in my wildest dreams did I think Pete was in mortal danger.

A sense of urgency began to consume him. He wanted to get the movie script written, and he wanted to pursue as many speaking engagements as possible. In fact, every moment in front of a group of people was a moment he embraced to share the gospel. It was his mission the last few months of his life.

When we attended a book signing in Westwood, the neighborhood most famous for the campus of UCLA, Pete shared his story and his faith with everyone he met. Whether it was the bookstore owner, the cashier, or a fan wanting an autograph, Pete would tell them about how Jesus Christ had radically changed his life and how for the first time in his life, happiness had found him.

One particular young man gave Frank, Pete, and me a memory that we could never forget. In fact, we made it a point to frequently remind Pete of an incident he had with a teenager in the Westwood bookstore. A UCLA college freshman walked up to Pete and inquired about the stack of *Heir to a Dream* books sitting on the table.

"You wrote this?" the young man asked.

"I wrote it with my friend, here," Pete acknowledged me.

"Oh. And who are you?" the young man inquired of Pete.

The college student wasn't asking who I was. He was asking Pete who he was. Frank and I laughed as Pete graciously informed the college student.

"I'm Pete Maravich. I used to play professional basketball."

"What's the book about?" the young man asked.

"My life and my dad's life."

Frank and I moved away and had a good laugh at the Hall of Fame basketball legend trying to explain who he was to a clueless college kid. After a few minutes, we noticed Pete had left the signing table, and the young man and he were in a very intense but quiet conversation.

I knew exactly what was happening. Pete was sharing his faith with the young man, and the guy would most likely be cornered until Pete was finished. I had never known anyone like Pete. He was a dedicated Christian who was always compelled to tell the story of how he found happiness through Jesus. It was the most important thing of Pete's life, and he was never going to let an opportunity to share his story slip by.

Since there was no crowd at the store waiting for autographs, Pete had plenty of time to visit with the student. After several minutes, the young man left, and Pete turned to us with a strange look on his face.

"So, how did that go?" we asked.

Pete shook his head. "Pretty strange, actually."

"What happened?"

"Well, I was telling him about my faith, and things were getting really serious. The kid was hanging on every word about eternal life, death, hell, and his time to make a decision, and then finally the kid says to me, *Pete, may I ask you a question*? I told him he could."

"What did he ask?"

"It was a very deep and philosophical question," Pete replied with a wry smile. "The kid asked if I had eaten garlic for lunch."

Pete burst into laughter, and we joined in.

That young man's remark became one of our running gags with Pete when we felt he was getting too serious with us. We would ask him if he had eaten garlic for lunch, and that reminder would lighten just about every moment.

After the death of Press, Pete ramped up his schedule of speaking engagements, and his oratory had never been better. He was very compelling, and he could tell his life story in a concise and interesting way that mesmerized crowds.

As I mentioned in the last chapter, when he stood on the stage at a Billy Graham revival just twenty days after the death of Press, he became a sought-after public speaker. The nationally televised broadcast spawned requests from all over the country such as his appearance on the *700 Club* with Ben Kinchlow.

In Los Angeles, I had the privilege of sitting in on several interviews, including a Roy Firestone interview for his ESPN show, *Sports Look*. We met privately with journalist Scott Ostler, who at that time was working for the *Los Angeles Times*. Scott wrote a tremendous article for the *Times* sports page that was extremely complimentary to Pete and Press. On those two particular occasions, it was interesting to watch two sports reporters, who were at the top of their games, treating Pete with such respect and showing him the honor he deserved. Pete was magnificent on camera and in front of seasoned media professionals. He was a natural.

Also during this period, Pete appeared at a dinner party in Arizona in October of 1985. He was asked to speak during a beautiful affair at the home of Jimmy Walker, a prominent insurance agent who served many professional athletes. Glen Campbell was the special guest singer, and Pete was asked to share his testimony.

What occurred that night was simply amazing. The following paragraphs represent a few featured moments from the night that no one in attendance would forget. Pete walked up on the stage in front of the guests, and with their undivided attention he pulled no punches. He boldly stood in front of the strangers as if it would be everyone's moment of decision. He adjusted the microphone on the stand, and he launched into his speech:

*Jesus Christ changed my life. Money didn't do it,
women didn't do it, friends didn't do it, pastors didn't do it,
wealth didn't do it, success, being president of a company,
owning your own business, having your own boat, whatever
you can think of. That's not what I'm called to do. Wealth,
whatever you can think of, whatever is holding you back from
Christ, won't do it. Do you realize that if you live to be eighty
years old, you have only lived a little over 700,000 hours?
Half of those—350,000 hours—is spent sleeping and watching
television if you're the average person.* **I don't have much
time left.**

Yes, that was the moment caught on video where Pete
actually said that he "*didn't have much time left.*"

*And the time that I have, I'm giving it to Jesus Christ.
I'm giving it to Him because that's what I'm called to do. I'm
not called to come up here to be nice and speak in generali-
ties; "Pete, you might offend some people." That's fine.*

Pete looked around at the faces in front of him. He was
serious and determined, and then he continued:

*I feel compassion for people that I've never felt before.
Everybody I meet, I feel for, because you see, there is a heav-
en, and there is a hell. And I could stand up here, and I could
even talk to you about evolution for the next two hours if you
wanted to, but I don't need to do that. You can just go read Sir
Fredrick Hoyle of Cambridge, the foremost evolutionist and
mathematician and astronomer of our time, who just recently
said, "I have been duped for twenty years!*

*Through my mathematical experiments there is no
possible way that we came from primordial soup. In fact, I
know we have been created. You can call it God. I don't. But,
we have been created from something."*

Pete continued.

213

"And yet, our kids in school every day are taught that exact thing. And by the time they get out of school, they're taught twelve thousand hours of evolution and secular humanism. But, you know, Hell is a real place, folks. Did you know that as we've been here, literally thousands of people have died? Between eighty-four and ninety-four people die every minute in the world. Two million people died last year in the United States. Thirty million people died last year in the world. Thirty million people died last year! Of those, conservative estimates by theologians and Christians say that over ninety percent are in the abode between death and judgment. They're there. It's real. You're spiritual. You're going to live forever— you got nothing to do with it. So am I. I praise God I know where I'm going. And I hope you do too, Pete warned as he stopped and scanned the faces in front of him.

I hope tonight you will look at yourself—examine yourself. Are you really happy? Because, Hell's not a good place to go, and Jesus talked about Hell more than He talked about Heaven. God doesn't want anyone to go to Hell. And, here we are with our finite little minds, with three percent use of our brain saying, "There is no God!" We have an expanse of a universe here, and nobody knows where it goes. The atheist says there is no God out there. How can any man say that? How can any fool believe it? You know what they do in Hell? I'm sure a lot of you would like me to get this over with. There's going to be a lot of weeping in Hell, and there's going to be a lot of wailing. There's gnashing of teeth—probably because of anger, or probably because they know that they have been separated from God forever.

If the non-believers in his audience weren't uncomfortable by this moment in his speech, they were about to be.

214

There's isolation, and there is spiritual blackness.
There's no light in Hell. Absolutely no light! There have been
testimonials from people who have died and come back—
testimonies from non-religious scientists. Dr. Kubler-Ross,
who spent her last twenty-five years on death and dying, she
went before a thousand doctors in Los Angeles not too long
ago, and she got a standing ovation when she declared that
there is life after death. And, she's not even religious!

Pete studied his audience again and saw familiar faces.
There were other retired professional players in the audience—
men he had competed against, such as Paul Westphal, Neal
Walk, and Garfield Heard. The speech he delivered was much
more important than any game he had ever played against the
men sitting in front of him.

Not only is spiritual blackness there, there are two
things here that won't be in Hell. There are two things that we
depend upon here—one of them is light. You see these lights?
Light. It gives you mental stability. Nobody likes to be in the
dark for long periods of time. The other thing we need is some-
thing to grab onto—solid things. Material things. Hell's a bot-
tomless pit. You don't grab anything there.

This part of his speech reminded me of our very first
meeting when he asked me if I thought his mother was in hell.
Pete was not afraid of talking about its reality, and his audience sat completely silent as he drove home his point.

You can spend ten, twenty, thirty, forty, fifty thousand
centuries in Hell and never accomplish one thing there. And
you'll know that you don't have one less second to spend there.
I cry at night for people I don't even know. I cry for my broth-
er. I pray for him constantly.

This was the Pete I had come to know. He loved to
share the hope he had inside and he could go on all night.

215

"You'll never prove God, although all of the evidence is there. In fact, I probably could prove Him to you from the research I've done. But, you don't need the proof from me. You've got the atheists, the evolutionists, the biochemists, the nuclear scientists; they've all collected their evidence. They've all fallen flat on their faces. Of course, you don't read about any of that."

And then Pete moved into the part of his talk that always meant the most to him. He wanted to make sure his audience knew the way to find the truth he had found.

I hope and pray that any of you who have never had a relationship with Christ ... it's not important that you know who Christ is, it's important that He knows you. Matthew 7:23 says, "I never knew you, depart from me, you who practice lawlessness." Everybody knows who Christ is, especially in America. You can walk that tight rope, and you can be just like me. For every person who is just like me, you have a testimony. There are literally tens of thousands in the pit of Hell. One day, mark my words from my heart; you'll be standing there in front of the Judge of the universe. Don't say, "I've got time. I can do it tomorrow; I can do it next week." You don't have any time. He gives you today. Your life ends when it ends. There's no coming back. Examine yourself. Think about it. Give Christ a chance. I guarantee you; you will literally be a totally different person. When you receive Jesus Christ into your life, He will do something to you just like He's done to me.

Pete concluded. I'm sure the smartly-dressed guests and the hundred or so underprivileged youth who received free bicycles that night, would agree that they had never heard such a dinner speech. Pete vowed he would utilize the remainder of his life talking about the change he had experienced in his life because of Jesus Christ. Pete didn't miss that opportunity.

CHAPTER 20
Hollywood Memories

When I went into business with Pete, one of my proudest moments was to see my name next to his on our book, *Heir to a Dream*. The next proud moment for me was to write my name near his as we appeared together at book signings. Next, was the moment I completed my first draft of the screenplay *The Pistol: The Birth of a Legend*, and the story credit had Pete's name next to mine.

Today, one of my prize possessions is the first draft of the screenplay with Pete's handwritten notes on the pages. When Pete came to Hollywood for his next-to-the-last time, Frank, Pete, and I conducted our script writing sessions at the Beverly Garland Hotel on Vineland Avenue in North Hollywood. It was a block from my apartment, and it was convenient for me to walk over to the hotel in the mornings and join Pete for hot breakfast. For lunches we had to find a health food store so Pete could order a turkey and bean sprout sandwich.

The writing sessions at the Garland were helpful as Pete described his childhood story the way he wanted it told on the big screen. As Frank and I sat on the chair and sofa, Pete stayed on the bed and leaned against the pillows. His long legs were stretched the length of the mattress.

"I just got a stress test, and everything checked out fine, the doctor told me. They think I might have neuritis, which is causing this pain in my shoulder," Pete explained with a wince.

As we continued working our way through the pages of *The Pistol* screenplay, I looked at Pete, and his eyes were closed. He rubbed the front of his shoulder, and I could tell he was in pain.

"Pete? You want to take a break?" I asked.

"No, I'm okay," he attempted to assure us.

I glanced over to Frank, who was obviously as concerned as I was.

"The docs told me that the bone cancer Dad had was the worst kind of pain anyone could endure. When I feel this pain in my shoulder, I just think of what Pop went through, and I stop feeling sorry for myself. Seriously, the doctors gave me a clean bill of health. Where were we?"

Our meeting that day ended, and as I sat in my home office, I pondered how much things had changed in the previous six months. It hadn't been that long ago that Pete and I were hitting golf balls at the Weddington Golf and Tennis facility in Studio City. Pete wanted to show off his golfing skills one afternoon. We bought a bucket of golf balls, and having played hundreds of rounds in high school and college and through most of my married life, I was very confident in my ability to hit a long, straight ball on the range. My confidence quickly wavered when Pete stepped up to his first ball sitting on the rubber tee. He crushed the drive over three hundred yards and as straight as a string.

"I really like to play golf. I just don't have the time," Pete quipped as he teed up another ball.

He adjusted his stance, executed a nice slow backswing, and smashed another drive up the middle and the same distance as the first ball.

I've always thought that there are at least two sports that turn some professional athletes into circus clowns ... one is tennis, and the other is golf. You can put an NFL, or MLB player, or for this argument a 6'5" NBA guard on a golf course and get a good laugh at his clumsiness and inability to get a clubface to properly strike a golf ball.

218

That wasn't the case with Pete. I got the impression he could have become proficient in any sport in which he wished to excel.

"What other sports do you think you could have shined in, Pete?"

"Baseball, I think," Pete answered without hesitation.

"You look like a Randy Johnson-type pitcher," I agreed.

"My dad stopped that desire in its tracks early on. He took me out in the backyard of our house when I was just a little guy. My friends were all going to the baseball field and having fun, so when I told Dad I wanted to be a baseball player as well as a basketball player, it made him uncomfortable. I know this is going to sound a little abusive, but Dad took me in the backyard, and he hit a baseball as high as he could so I could track it down and attempt to catch it. It didn't take long for me to misjudge the ball, and it hit me directly on my face! I cried like a baby, and during my whimpering and tears, Dad told me how much better it would be to concentrate on basketball like he did when he was a kid. Those words stuck in my mind, and I never played baseball again."

There are so many wonderful moments with Pete that remain fixed in my memory. One was when he called Frank and me to tell us he had secured us tickets for a Los Angeles Laker game. He gave us an address where he was hanging out until game time, and he instructed us to meet him there.

The address I heard was unfamiliar to me because it was located in an area we Ozarkians would call "tall cotton." We were to meet him at 1143 Summit Drive, in San Ysidro Canyon, Beverly Hills. When we arrived, we were welcomed into the home of Jerry Buss, owner of the Los Angeles Lakers.

As cool as that was, being a film buff and movie industry professional, I was more astonished that the iron gates we had just driven through opened to eighteen of the most famous acres on the planet. In 1919, movie superstar Douglas Fairbanks bought the old hunting lodge for his bride-to-be, silent film star Mary Pickford. Frank and I were driving up the private drive of "Pickfair," a twenty-five-room mansion overlooking Hollywood.

The property had servant quarters, tennis courts, and horse stables. It is said that the mansion may have been the first private dwelling in Los Angeles with an in-ground swimming pool. As the housekeepers, or security guards, or whomever they were welcomed us to where Pete was waiting for us in the main living room, the beauty of the interior architecture captivated me. This country boy was standing in the palace of the former king and queen of the Hollywood film industry, and surrounding me were walls of stunning mahogany, with beautiful parquet floors. Gold leaf and decorative trim adorned most of the rooms.

"Do you have any idea where you are?" I quizzed Pete.

"Jerry's house."

"No. No, you're not. This is Pickfair! Mary Pickford and Douglas Fairbanks's house."

"That's what someone mentioned earlier."

"Pete, Mary Pickford and Douglas Fairbanks started a company called United Artists with Charlie Chaplin and D.W. Griffith. This is unbelievable. This is a historical place, Pete. Pickford and Fairbanks were the first royal couple of Hollywood," I told him.

"Hmmm. Whatever you say. I'll show you around."

In typical fashion, Pete wasn't impressed.

"Jerry's going to meet us at the Forum for the game," Pete mentioned slyly, knowing that I was thrilled to be in the home of the owner of the Los Angeles Lakers.

What followed was like a tour out of a dream for me. I was not a Pickfair expert, but I knew enough about the famous place and enough film history to be completely overwhelmed by the aura of my surroundings. I walked around the glorious mansion where all the truly great Hollywood parties took place in the 1920s and beyond.

During the roaring twenties and tumultuous thirties, the mansion was where the who's who of entertainment, industry, and government gathered in Los Angeles. If a person were anybody in the arts, politics, or science, they were most likely invited to Pickfair to socialize and hobnob with the rich and famous. If one weren't invited, it would be an indication he or she hadn't cracked the hard shell of the closed Hollywood community. When Charlie Chaplin is the next-door neighbor and a business partner, one knows they are part of an elite group.

Film stars such as Gloria Swanson, Joan Crawford, and Greta Garbo were rubbing elbows with world leaders such as the Duke and Duchess of Windsor, Lord Mountbatten, President Franklin Roosevelt, Eleanor Roosevelt, and the queen and king of Siam.

Other notables were people such as Albert Einstein, Babe Ruth, Amelia Earhart, Marconi, Charles Lindbergh, Thomas Edison, Noel Coward, and Helen Keller to name a few.

In 1976, the Academy of Motion Picture Arts and Sciences honored Mary Pickford with an Honorary Academy Award for her work in the film industry.

I found myself sitting in the formal living room right where she sat when she said "thank you" to a national television audience. That telecast was a very rare opportunity for the rest of the world to see Mary Pickford and the interior of the famous Beverly Hills home. Not only had I seen that telecast, I was suddenly on that "set!"

Our tour continued out a back door, and as we walked down the sloping hill toward the swimming pool, I could almost hear the laughter and music of one of Pickfair's famous parties in the 1920s. The view of the City of Angels was like nothing I had seen since living in L.A. It was truly like a scene from a movie.

A few hours later I found myself walking into the Fabulous Forum, where the owner of Pickfair as well as the Los Angeles Lakers, Jerry Buss had seats waiting for us. I had been to several Laker games before, but on this special occasion I was attending as a guest of the owner and as a friend of NBA star Pistol Pete Maravich.

Okay, our seats admittedly weren't the half court seats where Pete was sitting, but we were only about twelve rows behind him and happy to be in the building. Pete smiled at us and indicated that his seat was much closer to the action.

After the game I experienced what it is like to be with a superstar who is around other star athletes. After watching Magic Johnson, Kareem, and the other Lakers win another game, we went back to the locker room area with Pete, and he introduced us to some of the players as they came out to shake his hand.

It was during those moments I realized the impact Pete had on many active members of the NBA.

The Lakers of the 1980s were a dynasty and had every reason to be proud of who they were and what they had accomplished, but all that diminished when they saw "Pistol Pete" standing in the hallway.

The Laker players were fans much like me. They shook Pete's hand and thanked him for coming to the game. We visited with A.C. Green, Michael Cooper, and Magic—or, should I say, Pete visited with them. Frank and I stood there like groupies, shaking hands and smiling. We were just happy to be breathing the same air.

The spring of 1987 held a few more memories for me. Pam and I were members of a church in Van Nuys, California that was pastored by one of the brightest men I had ever had the pleasure to befriend. Dr. Jess Moody was a man who loved people, his church, and being a part of the Hollywood community. He was a great author, orator, preacher, and his humor and candor kept his congregations engaged. We had the privilege of working with Jess and his staff for nearly ten years, and he and his wife, Delores, were our neighbors when we lived in Chatsworth, California.

Pete told me that he wanted to visit our church on a Sunday to hear Jess Moody preach. That morning turned out to be memorable for many reasons. First of all, our friend Tom Lester, best remembered for playing the role of Eb Dawson on the television show *Green Acres*, was attending church that morning. When Pete and Tom met, there was an immediate familiarity as if they were old college buddies from the South. They could have passed for brothers. Both were tall and thin, and their hairstyles were the same. When they conversed, Tom's Mississippi accent and Pete's Carolina-Louisiana accent and rhythm of speaking bonded them even more.

As I was writing this chapter of the book, I casually mentioned to my son Casey that we were fortunate to have cast Tom Lester to appear as Adult Pete in the beginning of *The Pistol: The Birth of a Legend*. He was shocked to learn for the first time that the tall guy walking through the gym in the beginning of the film isn't Pete Maravich. For thirty years he believed that was Pete playing himself in the movie's prologue. Casey was just a baby when Pete met him and held him for the first time. It was a bit sobering to explain to him the chronology of events and remind him that Pete never got to see the film produced.

Pete's instant friendship connection with Tom Lester inspired us to write the aforementioned prologue to *The Pistol*, which sets up the entire movie. As "Pete" walks into an empty gym with his son, he says that he would like to take his son back in time to where his story began. Frank, Rodney Stone, and I wanted that to be Pete playing himself. Sadly, that opportunity never happened.

When I watched the scene unfold on the set, it was almost too difficult to witness. It was a moment we had talked about, and we wished so much that Pete could have been on camera playing the role. Thankfully, Tom Lester was terrific in the part, and those on the set who knew Pete personally were emotionally moved by his portrayal.

We looked back and realized how fortunate we were that Pete requested we attend church on that spring morning in 1987. Tom Lester and Pete's meeting in Van Nuys was an unexpected treat, and little did we know on that Sunday morning that it would be their last encounter.

Frank insisted that we cast the lead in *The Pistol: The Birth of a Legend* using an actor from Louisiana. He wanted to find and hire a young boy in his home state as a tribute to Louisiana and also to show potential investors that the movie would be "home grown" to a great extent.

A little bit of Hollywood came to Baton Rouge as we secured the Assembly Center on the campus of Louisiana State University for our movie auditions. Having been to a few cattle calls in New York City and Los Angeles, I wasn't surprised to see dozens of twelve-year-old wannabe actors entering the building. Pete sat with us behind an eight-foot-long folding table as we prepared ourselves to find the perfect match for a young Pete look-alike.

The challenge for us was daunting. We wondered if it would be wiser to find an athlete we could mold into an actor, or to cast a young actor whom we could mold into a proficient basketball player. That challenge was a discussion we had many times as we looked for talent and ramped up to production. If you asked a basketball coach which way he would go, I'm sure he would say to find a gifted athlete and give him a few lines if one is concerned with authenticity.

The actor and director side of me was challenged because I knew that a good actor could create the needed emotion we wanted on the screen. All the great basketball moves in the world can't make up for bad acting.

One by one, the children wishing to be cast as young Pete Maravich filed into the arena. The few dozen prospects quickly grew to a few hundred. We decided to line up several kids at a time, four rows deep, and then put them through a series of drills. With Pete Maravich sitting at the producer's table, we were relying heavily on his judgment.

Pete had never cast a movie before, but after coaching hundreds of summer basketball camps, he had a keen ability to immediately spot athletic talent and the body type we needed for the film.

As the kids continued to line up, the parents of the hopeful child actors began filling one side of the arena seats. Before long, there were hundreds of parents and relatives looking on as their children auditioned.

One of the more humorous things that caught us off-guard was how many young girls auditioned for the part. It was one thing to see kids who were too old or too physically different. Some were way too short. Some were way too tall. When we noticed African-American girls auditioning for the part of the young Pete Maravich, it encouraged us to see just how excited the public at large was to be involved in a movie about our sports hero!

I came to the conclusion that many of the people in the stands who had accompanied their children to *The Pistol* auditions were "Pistol Pete" fans like me. They wanted a glimpse of their basketball hero. They also figured they might get to shake his hand or exchange a word with the basketball legend.

As the audition continued through the day, a dark-headed kid with a determined look in his eyes stood out to Pete.

"That kid with the dark hair," Pete commented to me. "That's what I looked like in the eighth grade."

I watched the boy dribble behind his back and between his legs as instructed. Many of the kids were proficient as Frank gave them instructions, but Pete was locked in on the dark-headed boy.

"His name is Adam Guier," we informed Pete.

"If he can act at all, that's the kid," Pete assured us.

226

As the producer of the film, I was trying to pare down the dozens of good prospects to a handful, but Pete was already settling in on one boy. After the actors and actresses finished the skills test of the audition, they filed one by one into the stands to sit with their parents. We wanted to address them all and tell them what to expect next in the casting process. And then, something unexpected happened.

Again, allow me to preface this by saying that I had been to a hundred auditions in my life, but what was about to happen would set a new standard in my entertainment career. Frank introduced Pete to the adoring crowd of parents and children, and the ovation was huge. That was a first for me—an ovation at an audition. Pete took the microphone from Frank and thanked the parents for taking time out of their busy day to bring their kids to the audition. He thanked the kids for their interest in being in the film. After a minute or two of informing the crowd of the story we hoped to tell on film, Pete suddenly changed the subject.

"All I wanted in life was to be the greatest basketball player to ever play the game," he began. "I wanted to be the first million-dollar professional in the NBA. And, I wanted to win a big championship ring that proved to the world that I was one of the greatest."

It was the start of a speech we had heard a few times, but then the captive crowd got something they never expected. Pete began to preach. My church-going friends might say, *Pete was sharing his testimony*, but in reality he launched into a sermon that the folks in the arena would never forget.

"I had honorary admiral status in the Navy, I was the first million-dollar rookie, I had fancy cars and houses, and I used to carry five thousand dollars in cash in my wallet so I could give it away and feel good about myself," he began.

227

Pete liked to start his talks in that fashion because the accolades and things he had achieved were impressive to almost anyone of any age.

"I studied Eastern religions. I meditated. I even believed a UFO would pick me up one day. I looked for happiness in everything I could think of. In basketball, I set records that may be around for decades, but none of that brought me happiness. I searched for happiness all my life and couldn't find it, but when I found Jesus, happiness found me."

Frank and I exchanged a look. What was happening? Our Hollywood audition had just turned into a revival service, and Pete was the evangelist. I felt a sense of embarrassment, and my selfish pride began gnawing at me. I was a professional in show business, trying to produce my first motion picture, but with the news media in every corner of the room, my very-professional-talent-audition had been transformed into something resembling a tent revival.

In retrospect, Pete was nothing short of amazing. His appeal to the crowd was direct and clear. His improvisational sermon turned into one of the most moving and emotionally charged twenty minutes of my life. Some in the audience were wiping tears from their faces, some were nodding, and many were hoping that their children were taking Pete's advice to heart. He encouraged them all to attach their dreams to a higher, less selfish calling.

His words also impacted me. I had to stop and reassess my priorities. Life is short and full of self-satisfying pursuits that at the end of the day aren't as important or as beneficial to our well-being as we think they are. Pete had made a commitment to God and to himself that when given the opportunity to share truth, he would do it.

228

Pete was not a shallow man. His life at age thirty-nine had seen many trials and tribulations that shaped him into a man who cared about people and their souls. I have often said that Pete Maravich was a lot like the apostle Paul in the Bible. He had one major focus for the rest of his days on Earth—share the Good News with others.

"I know that boy," Frank told me as he pointed to the dark-haired kid who had impressed Pete in the audition.

Thirteen-year-old Adam Guier from Shreveport, Louisiana, was a friend of Frank's family. Out of the hundreds of children to audition for the lead role of "Pistol Pete," the boy somewhere in the middle of the pack stood out to Pete. Out of the hundreds of kids trying out, it was a shy-looking kid with a winning smile and exceptional dribbling skills who won the day. Once we all agreed on the choice, it was our goal to have the young actor work out with Pete on a weekly or monthly basis until we began principal photography on the movie.

Things were coming along nicely regarding the pre-production of the film. Frank was putting together a group of investors who admired Pete and his amazing story. The script was taking shape. Pete had picked the boy who would play him in the film, and we felt as if we were on track toward starting production.

Pete would never have the opportunity to personally coach and groom our star as we had planned. A few months later, I would return to Baton Rouge, but it wouldn't be to produce *The Pistol: The Birth of a Legend* movie. It would be to serve as a pallbearer at Pete's funeral.

229

CHAPTER 21
See You in L.A.

Pete's public appearances, both on camera and off, were stirring more public interest in the NBA's greatest showman. When his high school basketball jersey was retired in North Carolina, he accepted the invitation and loved the nostalgic trip back home. The special event gave him another reason to connect with people and to share his story.

Not a thousand rings ... not a hundred billion dollars would make me change where I am right now, Pete would tell anyone who would listen. What a privilege it was for me to travel around the country with him as we promoted our book, *Heir to a Dream*. The soon-to-be best-seller made it to retail shelves all over America, and Thomas Nelson publishers had high hopes for its success.

While Pam, Casey and I were vacationing in Missouri during the Christmas and New Year holidays, Pete asked me to join him in Oklahoma City on December 30th, where he was to be inducted into Oklahoma City's All College Tournament's Hall of Fame. The tournament is the oldest of its kind in the United States, and they wished to honor Pete for his outstanding contribution to the game and the tournament. They specifically wanted to commend him for his exciting 1968 performance, when Pete and his LSU teammates barnstormed through the winter tournament. Pete averaged forty-six points over three games and was awarded the Most Valuable Player trophy.

I saw the event as yet another unique opportunity for me to sign autographs alongside Pete, and better yet, I could bring my dad with me and introduce him to "Pistol Pete."

When Pete and I talked on the telephone, we agreed to meet at the arena in Oklahoma City, and I informed him that I would need a few more tickets for the game. Pete welcomed the idea of meeting more of my family, so I invited my dad, my brother, Doug, his son, Brandon, and my Uncle Bill Hunt whom we would pick up in Bartlesville, Oklahoma along the way.

Pete called my parents' house in Mount Vernon, Missouri, to leave a time and place to meet. When we arrived at the arena in Oklahoma City, Pete was there to meet my family entourage in the hallway. As I expected, he made a wisecrack about how I was the tallest member in my family.

Pete shook hands with my family, and I was particularly proud when I watched him shake my dad's hand. It was a moment that I had longed for since I had first met Press. I wanted my dad to befriend Pete and to close that circle, because over the years spent with Pete, I had told him many of my father's WW2 stories. Pete was fascinated by my father's acts of heroism in France, Belgium, and Germany. I was so proud of my father, and I wanted Pete to understand the honor I held for his father and for all men and women who serve our country in the military.

"Darrel brags about you all the time," Pete informed my dad as they shook hands.

"I hope he says all good things about me," Dad replied.

"Mostly good," Pete laughed and assured him. "You guys ready to watch some basketball?"

Meeting Pete was a special moment for my family. They were fans of his sports legacy and had listened to the many stories I had shared with them over the last few years about my time with Pete and Press.

231

For Pete, it was another opportunity to share his testimony with another audience. He didn't see another time of recognition as an honor or a pat on the back for himself. In Pete's thinking, the night was about his relationship to people who wished to see him in person, meet him, and seize the opportunity to shake his hand. Also, being inducted into another hall of fame was a fresh opportunity for him to share with the world that he was a changed man, privileged to have lived life on the edge and to have survived because of God's grace and purpose for his life.

Fans attending the tournament were given the chance to purchase books in the arena and meet the authors. Pete and I sat at a table and wrote personalized messages into the first pages of *Heir to a Dream*. I knew that the tournament attendees hadn't come to see me or to get my name scribbled in their books, but regardless, Pete graciously made sure I signed every book that he signed. As the line moved by, he introduced me to each of his fans and told them that he and I were making a movie together. Again, pride swelled in my chest as my childhood sports hero was honoring me in front of his adoring fans. Pete's humility was on full display once again.

During the induction ceremony, Pete respectfully made his way to center court, where he was introduced to the cheering crowd and honored with a plaque. The standing ovation from the fans in attendance was inspiring. It was clear that the Oklahoma audience was thrilled to welcome the legendary NBA Hall of Famer back into their presence.

Pete enjoyed the accolades, and he humbly thanked everyone for the applause. Once again he seized the special moment to deflect any praise he was given back to Press and to God because it was his earthly father and his Heavenly Father who had made his success in basketball a reality.

232

"Words cannot explain the bond that occurs when a father teaches his son the important things he has learned in life," Pete addressed the audience. "My father opened up the past and related the ways in which he mastered his vocation, but he also shared what he had learned while enduring the pitfalls. It was a dream that would rescue him from the life paths that his father and grandfather had walked … a dream that would elevate him from a common existence to a place of happiness and security. My dad's vision was based on the excitement of basketball and the enthusiasm he had for the game. When I came along, my dad's dream included me."

Pete and I sat in the stands for the rest of the game, and periodically fans would walk up to where we were sitting to ask Pete to autograph our book. After Pete scribbled his classic "Pistol Pete" and a favorite Bible verse onto the page, he graciously handed the book to me so I might sign as well.

"This is Darrel Campbell," Pete explained. "It's my story, but Darrel wrote it all," Pete nodded at me as he assumed his humble role.

When the tournament games concluded that night, we left the arena and headed to a restaurant nearby. We secured a nice table for the six of us, and as usual, the wait staff recognized Pete and seemed to go the extra mile to please.

"Uh-oh," Pete exclaimed as he suddenly recalled something troubling.

"What's the matter?" I asked.

"I don't remember what I did with the plaque the tournament gave me."

"Wow, it was such a big honor that you forgot to take the plaque home with you," I laughed.

"Maybe they'll find it and send it to me," Pete said.

"Or, maybe some fortunate fan just got themselves some Pistol Pete Maravich memorabilia," I nodded.

We had a good laugh that he had traveled such a distance for the honor and the plaque, and he was suddenly going home to Louisiana empty-handed. Dinner for us ended, and we all walked to the parking lot to say our goodbyes.

"I'm coming out to California to do a radio interview with Dr. James Dobson."

"Great. Let's get together after your interview. Bring your notes for the movie, and we can go through them together," I reminded him.

"I wrote all my thoughts on my script," Pete said. "You can copy them."

"Okay. Call me and tell me where you want to meet. Thanks for everything. Tell Jackie and the boys hello for me. Oh, and thanks for the Billy Graham book."

"Read it. It's good," Pete encouraged.

The Billy Graham book that Pete gave me was entitled *The Holy Spirit*. The book contained a personal note. Pete's stationery read:

From the desk of Pete Maravich:
Hang in there, brother. GOD is in control. Seek HIM with all your heart. We send our love to the three of you
– Peter & Jackie.

"Be careful. See you in a few days," Pete reminded me as he gave me a hug.

We shook hands, and I replied, "Have fun on Dr. Dobson's show. See you in Hollywood."

Those were the last words Pete and I said to each other. It was the final hug and handshake we would share.

CHAPTER 22
"I Feel Great!"

"Show me a hero, and I'll write you a tragedy."
- F. Scott Fitzgerald

My plane was delayed by bad weather, which is often the challenge of flying into or out of the Midwestern United States during the winter. I got into Los Angeles late on January 4, 1988. It had been an awesome trip. I got to spend time with my family, attend book signings, and witness Pete's induction into the All College Tournament Hall of Fame.

My father, my brother Doug, his young son Brandon, and my Uncle Bill would never be the same after our time together in Oklahoma City. As always, Pete had made lasting impressions on the people with whom he came in contact. He certainly made a huge impression on my family, and I know he thrilled the OKC Tournament fans. As far as I know, the award given to Pete that night was never found, so out in the world somewhere, there exists Pete's Hall of Fame plaque, if someone reading this book wishes to track down some valuable hidden memorabilia.

Before the days of cellular phones, I had to be in my home or office to receive a telephone call. It's hard for young people these days to grasp the challenge of finding pay phones outside convenience stores and supermarkets in order to make a telephone call in Los Angeles. If the public pay phone was not being used, I had to hope that I had enough change in my car ashtray to feed the telephone all the quarters or dimes it required.

I hadn't been informed yet where we were to meet for the script session, and because I didn't want to miss the phone call from Pete or Frank, I was determined to stay home and close to the telephone. We were to meet that morning to put the final touches on the shooting script, and I looked forward to incorporating Pete's new notes and thoughts into my master document.

I later discovered that Pete and Frank had scheduled a pick-up basketball game with Dr. James Dobson and some of his staff before the interview on Dr. Dobson's *Focus on the Family* radio program. Pete was thrilled about the opportunity to share his story with thousands of radio listeners, and I know he was looking forward to spending quality time with Dr. Dobson. After the pick-up game, Frank was to call me and tell me where to meet Pete and him for lunch. Each time Pete had come to Los Angeles in the past, we had managed to do something fun and memorable, and I hoped that this visit would be the same.

The phone rang.

"Hello?" I answered.

"D, it's Frank," the quiet voice on the other end of the line informed me.

"Hey, Frank. What's up? I've been waiting for your call. Where are you guys?"

There was an odd silence on the other end of the telephone line.

"Frank?" I questioned to break the strange silence.

"It's Pete. We're at St. Luke's Hospital. We were playing a pick-up basketball game with Dr. Dobson."

His voice halted a bit, and I heard a nervous tone in Frank's voice I had never heard before.

236

Before he could say another word, my mind went immediately to Pete's surgically repaired knee. I was certain he had hurt himself again and we would have to call off our script meetings. Admittedly, I was utterly selfish at that moment.

"Did he mess up his knee? Is he okay? What happened?" I asked innocently.

It was the first thing that came to my mind, and those were the first words out of my mouth. Frank's reply to my otherwise innocent question forever changed my life.

"D. Pete's dead."

Words can't do justice to the strange and overwhelming feeling that took over my entire body. It was like a rush of blood from my feet to my head and then a hollow feeling inside. I couldn't speak for a moment. It was like those moments when I played baseball and received a fastball blow to my batting helmet. For a few seconds everything shuts off. After a moment my words finally formed.

"No, Frank. He died? How? What happened?"

"He just collapsed on the court, D. He was dead when he hit the floor. I can't talk right now. I need you to come to St. Luke's and speak with the media. I'm by myself. Please. Hurry."

"I'm on my way," I assured him.

I hung up the telephone and stared out the kitchen window of our second story apartment. Suddenly I was overcome with emotion.

"Jesus! No!" I cried as I tried to keep from hyperventilating. "No! This isn't happening! This is a bad dream. No, Lord Jesus!"

My knees thumped against the kitchen floor as I knelt down. My mind was swirling wildly as I attempted to grasp the reality of the stunning news.

Struggling emotionally and physically, I tried to pull myself together to do what I had been asked to do. For a few more seconds, I couldn't think straight. It was as if my mind was processing sentence fragments in a world of long paragraphs. Although it had been years since my best friend Roger's tragic death, I had the same hollow feeling overwhelming me. It was as if memories from my past and hopes of my future were violently colliding into my present. Where I knelt on the floor was where Pete had been standing weeks before.

With tears in my eyes, I looked up to see our baby swinging in the mechanical swing that I used each day to keep him happy as I worked. I stood and extracted Casey from the swing, and I held him tightly.

Pete's voice echoed in my mind, '*Casey Jack!*' *You gave your baby boy a movie star name*!

"*Casey* because of baseball and *Jack* after his grandpa," I proudly explained.

With a name like that, he's going to be a star," Pete nodded.

I pulled Casey to my chest, and he laid his head on my shoulder. The poor baby had no idea what was happening, but all I knew was I needed to hold him close for my comfort. Again I was hit with the shocking reminder that life isn't always fair. Life is fragile, and every day must be used and enjoyed because there is no guarantee for a tomorrow.

I cried so deeply I couldn't make a sound.

As I held Casey and walked around the apartment, I struggled to gather my thoughts and collect my emotions. Instinctively I felt as though I needed his eyes to connect with mine to assure me that I could make it through another unexpected nightmare. Casey smiled the biggest smile as if to tell me, *life is still good*.

238

I gently returned Casey back to his baby swing and prepared myself for the first telephone call I had to make after receiving the shocking news. Sitting at my desk, I could feel and hear my heart pounding. The *click, click, click* of Casey's baby swing was the only sound in the apartment as I stared at my phone.

"Days," Pam answered the telephone at her office. "Hello?"

"Pam," I started, but suddenly had to stop as my throat tightened due to the emotion.

"What's the matter? Darrel! Is Casey okay? What's wrong?" Pam pleaded, filled with the instant panic most new mothers would experience.

"I need … you to come home as soon as you can. It's Pete," I struggled to reply.

"What? What's wrong?"

After a long pause, I choked through tears and finally replied, "He died."

"Died?"

"I've got to get to Pasadena—to the hospital as soon as you get home."

Pam was shocked to her core by the unexpected news.

"I'll be right there," she replied, trying to keep her emotions together.

I don't remember much after that. I hung up the phone, and I held Casey Jack as I waited. Across the room I saw the basketball on which Pete had written a sentiment to Pam, Casey, and me. It has been in my office now for over thirty years. Pete wrote:

"To Darrel and Pam and your boy. God bless you! Pistol Pete."

239

Twenty minutes had passed since my difficult phone call to Pam. Finally, the front door of our apartment squeaked open, and Pam walked in. Tears flowed down Pam's cheeks as she rushed to my arms. We held each other, and we cried.

I had to leave immediately but all I really wanted to do was hold Pam and Casey Jack. Memories of losing my childhood friend at age eighteen engulfed me again, and the heartbreak felt the same. As I embraced Pam, I felt a sense of comfort and experienced a strange sense of fear. I was a young man of faith, but the devastating blow of Pete leaving us forever sent a thought through me that I could suddenly lose Pam or Casey. Two of my closest friends had died suddenly and, in my opinion, prematurely, if there is such a thing.

As I drove to Pasadena with Rodney I turned on the car radio to listen to the inevitable. On nearly every radio station, reporters were breaking into regularly scheduled programs to announce the news that NBA superstar Pistol Pete Maravich had died suddenly of an apparent heart attack at age forty. After listening to several breaking reports, I turned off the radio and drove the rest of the way in silence.

Minutes later, we pulled into the parking lot of St. Luke Hospital in Pasadena. What should have been a beautiful day of camaraderie with my friends in Southern California turned into one of the darkest of days my life.

Just hours before Pete died, he had left his beautiful wife and young boys and flown to California to meet us. I had left my family and had flown in from Missouri to meet with him. We had many positive expectations for a productive week. According to our plans we should have been gathering at my apartment or having lunch with Dr. Dobson.

As Rodney and I walked into the emergency room entrance, I was greeted by the public relations representative of the hospital.

"You're Darrel Campbell?" she asked.

"I am," I replied with a nod.

"We've been waiting for you. I'm so sorry for your loss."

"Thank you," I replied.

Sorry for your loss, she said so robotically. *My loss?* Up to that moment I hadn't pondered how much Pete's death was a stunning blow for millions of fans and friends. But none of us who loved and admired the man could fathom the loss Jackie and the boys had suffered.

"We will gather the news media in this room as they arrive," the public relations woman gestured. "And we would like you to answer any questions that you wish. We'll have a doctor on hand to speak with them regarding any of the medical questions, but there won't be much they can say at this point. Are you comfortable doing this?"

"I suppose," I muttered as I tried to put words together. I felt as if I were acting in a movie, and I had suddenly forgotten my lines. It was surreal, but I was resolved to do my part.

"He's back here," the hospital representative informed me.

She said those sobering words as if she were taking me back to see Pete still alive. In my mind I was thinking, *No, he's NOT back there. My friend is not back there.*

Frank walked into the room. He was still in a state of unbelief. The woman led us to where Pete's body rested.

She opened a door to a room near where the doctors and emergency room personnel had been battling desperately to save Pete's life. Behind Frank I could see Pete's body lying under a sheet, but because of a partially drawn privacy curtain, I could only see from Pete's knees to his feet. Frank approached me in a slight state of shock. There were no tears, just halted words.

"What happened?" I asked.

"We played a pick-up game. We took a break to get a drink and Pete walked up to Dr. Dobson and said, *I need to play more often. I feel great.* And then, Pete just collapsed and hit the floor. They tried to give him CPR, but he was gone. He died in Dr. Dobson's arms."

"I can't believe this is happening," I said as I fumbled for words.

"Me either," Frank shook his head. "It's unbelievable."

I hesitated, not wanting to step behind the privacy curtain that separated me from my childhood hero. The nightmare was unfolding, and I really didn't want to be a part of it.

"I'm sorry, Frank," I continued, trying to find the right words.

There were no "right" words. We stood in silence. After a minute, Frank nodded that I should step around the curtain and see Pete. Seeing lifeless bodies has always been something I've avoided.

After a moment, I decided not to. At funeral visitations I'm not one of those who walk up to the casket to look at the deceased. It puts a final visual memory in my mind that often usurps the happy, smiling vision of the person I prefer to have in my head.

For some reason, a different feeling suddenly came over me. I wanted to see Pete, and I wanted to speak to him. It was Pete who told me that he had sat with the lifeless body of Press and conducted a one-sided conversation for several minutes after his father's death. Pete believed that the spirit of his father lingered in the room before leaving for Heaven. So that's what I wanted to do. I wanted to speak to him in case his spirit was lingering.

I stepped around the curtain, and although every fiber of my being didn't want to see him lying there, I forced myself to stand at his shoulder. He would have done the same for me. Pete's body was still, and a sheet was drawn up to his shoulders, leaving his face exposed for us.

"My brother," I whispered. "Pete. Come back to us."

I don't know why I said that, to be honest. Pete's body was cold, and his spirit had long departed. Tears rolled down my face, but I didn't want to lose control of my emotions in that room. I have no idea how long I stoically stood there gazing at Pete's lifeless expression. He was gone. My childhood idol and my friend had passed into eternity.

I recalled Pete's words he had said to me a few months earlier: *I will show up in Heaven, and my dad will be standing there to embrace me as if no time has passed. There is no time in heaven, D.C. No time. Just eternity!*

Pete painted a glorious word picture of a heavenly reunion, and I will never forget it.

Pops hasn't missed me for one second, D.C. He's in heaven with Jesus and his family and the angels. When I arrive, it will all be new for me, but not for him. I just hope that our Heavenly Father showed my mom mercy and that He welcomed her, too. I want to see my dad and mom together in Heaven. What an awesome day that will be!

243

The silence in the hospital room was deafening as I stood there.

"Your greatest desire is now your reality, Pete," I whispered to his lifeless body.

"Mr. Campbell?"

I turned to see the woman who had ushered me back to view the body.

"Yes, ma'am?" I answered.

"We really need you in the waiting area, Mr. Campbell. The media is here."

I walked into the emergency room waiting area where flashing photography lights and video cameras were instantly in my face. Reporters asked a flurry of questions, and again I felt as though my life in Hollywood had just become a movie. Oh, how I wished it were all a bad dream, but I was really standing there, and I was really being put on the spot for answers that fans across the world wanted.

"Why was Pete at the Nazarene church?"

"He was playing a pick-up game of basketball with Dr. James Dobson."

"What is your name?"

"Darrel Campbell. Pete and I wrote his new autobiography. We're planning to do a film as well."

"Had Pete been sick?"

"No. He is a health food guy, and he's been doing fine."

"So, you don't know of any drug use?"

"No way. No. Pete is a clean-living person."

"How old was 'Pistol Pete?'"

"Forty years old in June. He *was* forty," I suddenly corrected myself.

244

It was very strange to suddenly hear myself speaking about Pete in the past tense. But that was the hard fact I had to face. My hero, my friend, my business partner, and my mentor had just left the earth.

The questions from the hungry media continued until finally a doctor arrived to answer any medical questions. The public relations person stepped in to dispense other pertinent information to the press, and I slipped out of the room unnoticed.

"We need to go to Pete's hotel room and get his clothes and stuff," Frank informed me as I walked back into the quiet room where Rodney was waiting as well.

Packing Pete's clothing into his suitcase was a surreal fifteen minutes. The room seemed as still as his body lying in the hospital. I stared at a few things he had hanging in the closet area. I held the sleeve of one of his shirts in my hand and thought for a moment—*so, that's it?* We live our lives as best we can, and one day the breathing stops, the heart stops, and this flesh reaches the end of its earthly use.

That's it? I kept hearing those two words in my mind. In Pete's case, *"it"* was one of the most incredible lives ever lived. Still, that was *it*—like a star that burned brightly in the night sky and then one night its energy ended. The universe is left with only the memory of the star and where it once hung.

"They can't release the body and send him back to Louisiana until after an autopsy," Frank informed me.

"Why? He had a heart attack. What are they looking for?"

"He's a celebrity. Anybody famous, they have to find out exactly why he died. It's the law out here."

Rodney, Frank and I placed Pete's belongings in the back seat of Frank's rental car. As Rodney and I drove away from the hotel and back to our homes in the valley, we questioned everything. Without Pete in the picture, our future working plans seemed doubtful.

An article by Allan Parachini, a *Los Angeles Times* staff writer, mentions a mystery that has puzzled doctors for years regarding Pete's sudden death. He mentions that there is consensus that Pete had an extremely rare heart defect. It was a problem that may have been taken care of had Pete undergone bypass surgery, but at that time there was no way to detect his issue.

Pete's complaints at the Beverly Garland Hotel during our script session haunt me a little. *My shoulder is killing me.* On that day it seemed it was his physical pain mixed with the emotional pain of his father's death causing him discomfort.

"I just had a checkup," Pete informed us as he massaged his chest near his shoulder.

"What's it feel like?"

"It's strange. It runs through my shoulder. It's hard to explain. I was on the treadmill, and they said I had a touch of neuritis. They didn't seem too worried about it."

Pete winced again, and as I watched him closely, it was obvious that he was in a great deal of pain for a moment. Just as it came, the pain would leave him suddenly, and we would continue our conversation.

"I'm never going to complain about it. Not after watching what Pop went through. They say that there's nothing more painful than bone cancer. He was such a tough guy, and I just can't complain. I won't."

The Los Angeles County coroner eventually released Pete's body to be flown to Louisiana after a thorough autopsy that baffled many of the world's leading heart specialists. What puzzled the medical professionals most was how Pete Maravich was able to play basketball at all. He competed at the highest level, and on each of his teams he was on the court for most of the game.

"He's missing one of the major arteries to his heart," the doctors said.

Dr. Frank Litvack, a cardiology diagnostic expert at Cedars-Sinai Medical Center who reviewed the full documentary file, said that Pete's case is very bizarre. Litvack commented that the defect might be as rare as one in a million patients.

Other doctors were amazed that Pete had lived to be forty years old. Some specialists say that the heart rhythm Pete had usually leads to a sudden-death event by age nineteen or twenty. For over forty years, Pete's heart had been compensating by using a vessel that runs across the heart in order to supply the needed blood.

Under the file of *it's a small world*, Dr. Litvack, the renowned heart specialist who made the comments about Pete's "bizarre" malady, was the husband of Shelley Curtis-Litvack, Pam's boss at *Days of Our Lives*.

In bed that night, all was silent. Pam and Casey had fallen asleep after the long day full of emotion. The phone rang so constantly that I felt like taking it off the hook. People around the country and the world were stunned.

Because Pam and I had taken Pete to our church, our pastor and staff were also in mourning with us over the new friend they had lost.

As only Dr. Jess Moody could do, he gave a heartfelt tribute from his pulpit on Sunday morning. He celebrated Pete's life, and after bringing the congregation to tears, he offered us all hope as he reminded us all that Pete was enjoying his eternal life in Heaven.

I couldn't help but wonder if our dreams had come to a crashing halt. Fortunately, we had the *Heir to a Dream* book finished and on bookshelves around the nation. We had *Homework Basketball* produced and compiled into a four-tape video. But what would happen next? Was it really over?

Selfishly I thought of all the friendship, discussions and activities I had experienced with Pete. He had become the "phone call" guy in the relationship. He was the superstar with the personal phone book who could make a call to influential people and turn a normal day into an exceptional memory.

I remembered the first time we met. I recalled him kidding me about my height and wondering if I was tall enough to flush the toilet. I remembered his reaction as the German shepherd threatened him—our going to the Laker game, hanging out at Jerry Buss's Pickfair mansion in Beverly Hills, hitting golf balls at the driving range. I recalled our first meeting when Pete saw me for the first time and thought I was a college student wanting his autograph.

Exhausted from all the emotion, I got out of bed and walked into our living room. I prayed for Jackie and Pete's sons. I prayed that somehow I could find the good in it all. I had never known anyone like Pete. He inspired me, and he befriended me. I asked God to help us all get through the tragedy.

CHAPTER 23
Pete's Goodbye

Pam and I made the somber trip to Baton Rouge, Louisiana—this time for Pete's funeral. As I moved through the sad days, it was as if I had entered a dark story that I didn't want to experience. Death respects no one. It doesn't care about the plans we have made or our dreams for the future. Death comes to the newest newborn or to the oldest person we know. The shocking realization for me was that death had arrived in the midst of the exciting momentum of the most epic point in my life.

On the plane trip from Los Angeles to Baton Rouge, I pondered the impact. I had to come to the realization that after one final heartbeat, our best-laid plans for Pete and Pistol Pete Enterprises could be over.

James Dobson shared with me how strange and shocking it was to be playing basketball one moment and then administering CPR the next. Pete took one last big breath, and that was it. Frank remarked to me that as humans, we can breathe into someone's lungs to try to revive them, but when that doesn't work, you realize the power of God. Only He can give the breath of life and sustain it.

I stared at Pete's body lying in the casket. Because Pete had talked so much about the afterlife, looking at his lifeless body only reminded me of how alive in Heaven he must be. My concern remained focused on Pete's family and how his sudden departure would drastically change their lives. You often hear the bereaved say things such as, *It isn't fair*, especially when the departed one leaves family and small children behind or when the deceased is a child.

I have come to the conclusion that words of true comfort in those situations are rarely heard by the hurting. The best I've come up with is, *I love you and I'm praying for you,* which is all I could say to Pete's widow, Jackie.

As a pallbearer, I found myself doing a quick mental inventory of the blessings I had received from the day I met Pete Maravich until the day I helped carry his casket to its final resting place. The dream of meeting my childhood sports hero had come true. That relationship brought with it Pete's remarkable father and his beautiful wife and two sons.

The news that Pete's autobiography *Heir to a Dream* was flying off the bookshelves in nearly every state should have been good news, but as one can imagine, it had the opposite effect on me. As much as I loved the book and was so happy it was completed, I didn't care about book sales. I wanted my friend back. I wanted the man who had drastically changed my life. Pete was to be the film's basketball advisor and producer alongside me. I wondered if the pursuit of a family film about Pete's childhood would be shelved.

Pete seemed to have lived his forty short years to the absolute fullest and I discovered along the way that I wasn't the only person he made feel like a close friend. Dozens of people like me felt that they knew Pete in a special way, and on the sad day of his funeral, they made their way to pay their last respects to his memory and to the family.

Like an actor playing a part in a tear-filled tragedy, I sat in the small chapel room at the mortuary and watched as people who knew Pete Maravich walked through to view his body. One man in particular caught my eye. Coach Dale Brown walked up to the casket and looked at Pete for a minute, and then he walked back to sit and visit with Frank and me.

Coach Brown offered his sympathies to us, asked about Pete's wife and boys, and then congratulated me on the success of the book. With Coach Brown there was never any small talk. He launched into a heartfelt personal tribute to Pete that will forever remain a wonderful memory.

"The greatest," Coach Brown said as he shook his head sadly. "Maybe the greatest offensive player the game will ever see."

Brown recalled our meeting at the arena with his players and Pete. He mentioned how well he thought Pete was doing that day and how happy he seemed. Like the rest of us, Coach Brown assumed Pete would be around for a long time to continue impacting us with his words of wisdom and inspiration.

The church was full of heartbroken people who found it hard to accept that their beloved Pistol Pete Maravich had died at such a young age. The deaths of friends or relatives can make us sad and shocked, but Pete's death made me feel robbed. It was as if someone had broken into my life and taken one of my most valuable possessions—one that could never be retrieved.

A member of the mortuary staff escorted us to the front row of the church to be seated. I was so honored to be one of the six pallbearers, and although there was a lot I could have shared about Pete during the memorial, I was glad I was not called upon. As moving as all the tributes must have been that day, to be honest, I can't remember much of them. During the funeral service I could hardly bring myself to turn my head to look at the casket. Pete was in a peaceful and eternal place and reunited with Press. That's all I could think of.

Pete's pastor and good friend, Reverend Rodney Wood, opened the service with prayer. Ray Jones sang one of my favorite songs, *It Is Well With My Soul*. Pete's friend, Reverend Alfred Young expressed his thoughts with a special reading. The eulogy was read by John Lotz, which must have seemed a bit surreal to him since only six months earlier he had done the same thing at Press's funeral. Dr. James Dobson delivered a moving tribute as only he could do. Mr. Jones sang one of Pete's favorite songs, entitled *We Shall Behold Him*—the song that was sung at Press's funeral. After the song, Pastor Wood offered closing remarks, and everyone sang a hymn.

After Dr. Dobson concluded his closing prayer, we carried Pete's casket to the back door and gently placed it into the hearse. Many of the people in attendance joined the long procession to the body's final resting place in Baton Rouge.

The graveside service was brief and as common as one might imagine. We stood reverently as last words were spoken and Pete's coffin was lowered into the grave. Strains of *Amazing Grace* pierced the chilly winds that day. And that was it. Like the day of his death when I packed his things, the silence and finality was palpable. Once again I heard the simple phrase in my mind—*that's it*.

Putting a positive spin on such an abrupt ending to a friendship wasn't easy. As the pain of losing Pete subsided through the years, his words of encouragement echoed in my memories. The wisdom he shared motivated me as a husband, father, and professional. His investment in me as a friend is what made him heroic in my life. Pete, his father, and my father are and always will be heroes of my faith—heroes of my life.

EPILOGUE

I think it is fitting that I wrap up the writing of this book after the twenty-third chapter. This story of one of the most famous players to wear number twenty-three is meant to be a tribute from me to him. The duration of Pete's impact on my life has now been nearly the length of his entire forty years on earth. In many ways that seems like a long time, but when you think in terms of an average life span, Pete's four decades were brief.

There are many men and women who knew Pete well and who had a friendship with him for many more years than I. I've read their quotations in books, and I've watched as others have been interviewed for documentaries and TV specials. I'm sure there are hundreds of former teammates, coaches, friends, and relatives who could sit down and pen thousands more "Pistol Pete" stories than I can. With a legacy like Pete's, it would not be hard to do. Honestly I wish more of his friends would write about Pete as a boy or what it was like to be his teammate or his friend, especially in the years before I knew him. To have known him personally meant being positively impacted in some way.

In short, Pete changed lives. I know he changed mine.

I made a choice many years ago to branch out from a career as a writer in daytime television to pursue a film career, and that decision was in large measure because I met "Pistol Pete." My view of the brevity of life and my commitment to work hard during my precious time on earth is due in large part because Pete inspired me.

When I say that he changed my life, I mean that he changed my thinking about how I consider individual days of my life.

My fresh outlook, inspired by my conversations with Pete, had a transformative impact. I think differently when I wake up in the morning. I've learned to work harder and to walk through each day with an attitude of thanksgiving. When Pete left to assume his heavenly citizenship, he left me a changed man. His positive spiritual imprint was forever upon me, and his legacy took on a whole new meaning.

After Pete died, it was my quest to continue our business journey in some fashion as if he hadn't left. All of the pieces were ready to be put into place so we could begin producing a movie about his legendary childhood. I had all the information I needed, including Pete's personal notes scribbled into the margins of my screenplay. Frank was passionate about seeking funding and directing his first full-length feature film in his beloved state of Louisiana. We had almost everything, but we didn't have Pete.

Discussions among the production team after Pete's death were never about how the film had faded away with his passing. It was quite the opposite. The conversations were about how to make the film a reality and homage to our friend. With Pete gone, Frank and I burned up the phone lines between L.A. and Baton Rouge as we agreed with even more determination that we would stay the course. We owed it to Pete, his family, and ourselves. Many of the stories Pete had shared and events I had written in *Heir to a Dream* had to be revealed on screen so the world could appreciate the man we had grown to admire.

Movies require hundreds of people and typically millions of dollars. We knew we could get people to come to be a part of such a special film production, but it would take the commitment of some like-minded investors in Louisiana to make it happen financially.

Frank called everyone he knew who could step up and help finance the project. As he was busy raising funds, we enlisted our old friend from the *Another Life* TV show, producer Peter Andrews, as well as my close friend Rodney Stone, who was working for Warner Brothers at the time. All agreed that the production would be a labor of love to honor our brother, Pete.

We pulled in as many favors as we could to find craftsmen and talent to make the film. We had a terrific director of photography named Randy Walsh, who brought his very capable Louisiana crew to the project. As producer, it was my job to strengthen the script as best I could and also to coax some professional people to be a part of the super low-budget film. Academy Award nominee Millie Perkins was Peter Andrews's sister-in-law and we all agreed that she was the perfect actress to play Helen. Fortunately, so did she as she happily agreed to star in the film. Our next challenge was to find the actor who could do justice to the role of Press Maravich. We made some phone calls, and I paid Nick Benedict a visit at his apartment in New York City to ask him if he would do us all a huge favor and take on the role. Nick and I had worked together as actors on the soap opera *Another Life,* and I had seen his range as a performer. Fortunately, he loved the script, and he dove into the part like a seasoned pro. The result was astounding as he assumed the part of the feisty Coach Maravich.

We were fortunate to have Pete Maravich at the casting table with us when we discovered Adam Guier, the talented young boy who portrayed young "Pistol Pete." Adam wasn't a professional actor at the time, but he was a kid who had the body type and demeanor of a young Pete. Better yet, he could dribble with the finesse one would imagine young Pete possessing at age thirteen.

255

When *The Pistol: The Birth of a Legend* was produced, the final product became a fulfillment of a dream for many of my friends in show business such as Rodney Stone, Peter Andrews, John Lewis, Tom Lester, Eddie Hailey, Christine Andrews Rylko, Brent Havens, Nick Benedict, and John Wade to name a few. It wasn't easy producing the movie and getting it completed without Pete's input and vision. We had always imagined having Pete on the set helping us with basketball sequences and watching over how we portrayed his childhood.

Although Pete wasn't on the set, his presence and influence was constantly felt. It wasn't in a strange or mystical way, but rather it was his unforgettable words of hope and creativity. Because of our devotion to him, we were compelled to produce the movie the way that Pete wanted it done. His strongest desire was to make a movie full of hope that would speak to multiple generations.

It's not a movie about me, it's a movie about hope, Pete said many times. For those of us who had the privilege of knowing Pete the last years of his life, it is no surprise that he didn't want the focus on himself. Ninety-five percent of the film has young Pete on the screen, and yet Pete still dreamed of the focus being on hope and not on him.

Because we set out to fulfill Pete's every wish, we spent hundreds of hours in postproduction making sure the story was solid and making certain that the basketball sequences looked authentic. Frank was a stickler that the entire game atmosphere had to be genuine because he knew that Pete would have demanded realism. Every pass and every shot had to be as close to perfect as possible.

We refused to have Adam shoot the ball and then have the audience see a tight shoot of the basketball swishing through the net. If Adam missed a shot, we re-filmed the basketball sequence from the top of the scene.

At one point the production reached a tough financial spot and a major source of funding was needed. Producer Rodney Stone came to the rescue when he approached his dear friend Truett Cathy, founder of the Chick-fil-A fast food franchise. Cathy always had a big heart for young people, as well as a special place in his heart for Rodney. Truett Cathy also saw the opportunity to associate his growing company with quality family entertainment, so he immediately infused the production with a generous investment and kept our dream alive.

To honor the company and the man who helped us, the theatrical version of the film starts with Mr. Cathy standing in front of a theater marquee with a group of kids. He tells the audience that Chick-fil-A is a company that values clean family entertainment like *The Pistol: The Birth of a Legend.* After he welcomes the audience to the theater, Mr. Cathy walks into the theater with the children. It was a very novel way to start a film, and I believe Rodney Stone may have been the first film executive to integrate a sponsor into a movie like that.

Because of generous people like Mr. and Mrs. Truett Cathy and his children, Dan, Bubba, and Trudy, *The Pistol: The Birth of a Legend* played in theaters all across the southern USA and was distributed by Sony's Columbia/TriStar banner for home video.

Paul Rich, another close friend of Rodney Stone, picked up the title for his Rich International company and helped establish the foreign market strategy and sales.

Many years later, I still hear praise for the film. People of all ages tell me things such as, *"That's my favorite movie,"* or, *"My child has watched that film a hundred times,"* or, *"I have that film in my collection."* Some of my favorite comments regarding the film come from basketball fans and players who say things such as, *"I watched that movie before every game I played in high school."*

Another thrill Rodney Stone and I experienced was visiting the set of the *NBA on TNT* television show and seeing Charles Barkley hold up a DVD copy of our movie. Barkley looked into the camera and told his TV audience they should all get a copy.

Pete's friendship will always remain paramount in my story. Seventy-seven thousand-plus words in this book are the tip of the iceberg of the thousands more words I could have written about my hero and friend. Many memories and papers that remain in my safe deposit box still contain personal stories that will remain stored and private.

I started this book explaining how wonderful it was to befriend my childhood sports hero. The bucket list of contemporary heroes I wanted to get to know during my lifetime was a short one.

My list consisted of mostly entertainment and sports figures and unfortunately most of them are gone now: Bob Hope—an entertainer, Jack Lemmon—an actor, Ringo—a drummer, Ronald Reagan—a president, Carol Burnett—a comedienne, Tim Allen—a comedian, Jerry Lewis —a comic genius, Red Skelton—another comic genius, Lou Brock—a baseball player, and Pistol Pete Maravich—a basketball great. I met and befriended three on my list, Carol Burnett, Tim Allen, and Pete Maravich, and my life has been charmed beyond measure.

It's difficult to find oneself in a position to meet a personal hero, much less befriend them. For a kid from the Missouri Ozarks the odds were certainly stacked against me. Pete's path and mine divinely intersected. Pete had a desire to share his story. I was a writer. The timing was perfect. God's timing was perfect.

When Pete and I wrote *Heir to a Dream* and *The Pistol: The Birth of a Legend*, we talked a lot about how blessed we were to have fathers who were heroes. In both cases, our fathers were American heroes, motivating coaches, and inspirational influences. Our stories couldn't be more different if measured by the level of success in sports, but the journey isn't about sports: it's about all of us living all of life to our fullest potential.

This book evolved into a reminder that hero adulation can act as a kind of human mortar that holds societies together, because the icon one chooses to emulate is an example of success that one wishes to attain. Hopefully, our mortal heroes are men and women of character, whatever the chosen field. I want my children to find people who have blazed trails, and I want them to find beacons of hope and success that may light their paths.

Hero worship is a precarious concept because humans are fallible and should certainly never be deified. Humans will always stumble. They cannot be perfect. But their best qualities can be admired and followed. If a successful person like Pete Maravich can inspire others to become heroic and inspire someone else, the chain will continue. I'm pleased to say that Pete and Press found their ultimate champion to follow. After searching for happiness all their lives, the Maravich men both exited this mortal realm with a love for humanity that came from the example of Jesus Christ.

259

The last story I wish to place into this book about my hero and friend is based on a conversation I had just a few days before writing these words with Pete's pastor and friend, Rodney Wood. Rodney told me that two days before Pete's death, Jackie and Pete attended church as usual. It had been Pastor Wood's personal rule that he would never put Pete on the spot in church or draw attention to his family or him. Rodney wanted his small church to be a sanctuary for Pete to find peace from the outside world.

Part of Pastor Wood's Sunday morning preparation was to sit in one of the pews and pray before the service began. After his prayer, he looked back to see Pete and his family waiting for the church service to begin. Rodney went to Pete and shook his hand, just as he had done on many occasions. The following is how Rodney Wood told the story to me:

When I turned to walk away, there was an expression on Pete's face that made me stop in my tracks," Rodney explained. "I spun around and looked back at Pete. I asked, 'Are you okay, Pete?' Pete said he was fine. I continued to walk toward the front of the sanctuary, and I took my seat.

After a moment it hit me. I wondered if I should have in the past asked Pete to pray or speak in our church. Maybe I had taken my sensitivity toward his privacy too far. I got out of my seat, and I walked back to Pete and asked if he would close the morning service in prayer. At the end of the service, Pete prayed before our small congregation, and people couldn't say Amen enough as he spoke from his heart. It was common after the service for my wife, Becky, and Pete's wife, Jackie, to visit while Pete and I talked.

The kids and the four of us adults seemed to always be the last to leave, and I really enjoyed that private time I would get with Pete. He was so intense and always had something spiritual to impart to me. But on that particular Sunday, Pete simply told me he would be in L.A. working on a movie. Pete said, I'll see you in two weeks, or I'll see you in the air (meaning he would see his pastor in the rapture). That was the last time I saw Pete alive. I was so touched when Alfred Young, another friend of Pete's, told me he had talked to Pete on Sunday night, and all Pete could talk about was how I had asked him to pray in church. Pete was so honored; one would have thought that he had been asked to speak at another Billy Graham revival. Pete's humility is what I will never forget."

Author Marshall Terrill recently sent me a copy of those last few words that Pete spoke to his church and the fervent prayer Pete prayed. It is an intimate look at what was on his mind and heart just hours before experiencing his transition from life on Earth to his eternal life in Heaven:

I'd just like to share a few things. It'll take just a couple of minutes. As I was in the service this morning and listening to a beautiful song, "We Shall Behold Him," it really touched deep in the chamber of my own heart because that was one of the songs that was sung at my dad's celebration to go on to be with the Lord. That's the first time since I heard it eight months ago, and it really touched a chord in my heart. As I looked at my dad asleep in that coffin, I thought about when Paul said, "Absent from the body and present with the Lord."

261

I had to believe that, and that was really the whole message this morning as I trust in God because I know that the only work of God is that we trust Him. Before I can do the works of God in my own life, I know I must trust in Him and believe in Him and have an all-consuming thought of Him every day of my life. That's what I thought about when my dad laid there because it's so permanent. A peace came over me because I knew he was with the Lord. And I had to trust the Lord at that moment ... and I did. I also trusted Him two days ago when I was flying to Dallas. As we were flying in, all of a sudden we were flying into this very thick fog. I saw where the ground was just before we had descended into this thick fog at the airport. As we descended into this fog, it seemed to be a very long time because I knew we were coming closer to the ground. I found out later there was only a hundred feet of visibility. All of a sudden, the plane took off. I mean, it was amazing. The power hit, and we just went straight up. I don't know if he just missed the airport, or who knows? I'll know in eternity, I guess. But the thing that struck me at that moment was that if I took anything for granted in my life, in one moment I could be with Him.

I looked around, and I saw all of the other people on the plane. They were disgusted that we didn't land. Their thoughts weren't on Jesus Christ. Their thoughts were on making it to the Orange Bowl. They were going to miss their flight. There was a lot of laughing when we pulled up to our gate, of course. That's out of ignorance. But I just asked the Lord to forgive all of those people on that plane that I heard, for they were so blind. There was such a veil on their faces.

262

So, I think the message this morning is that we practice the fundamentals of the faith as I practiced the fundamentals of shooting a basketball and became good at what I did. We must practice our faith daily. We must pray, and we must praise Him. If you ever feel despondent or depressed, start praising God. You don't need to take two aspirin. If you want it to totally go away, just start praising Him. Praise Him in song. Praise Him for what He does, because we can live above our circumstances. We don't have to live in our circumstances. I've seen a lot of people in my life that are very Godly people, and I know those people have been hurt deeply in their lives before they could really walk in the Spirit of God. I just wanted to mention that.

Pete paused for a moment, and then he began to pray.

(Praying) *Father, I thank You so much for Jesus and Your Holy Spirit. Father, I just hope in the New Year that we could focus our sole attention on You ... that we could live above, as Paul said, that we will think into the heavenlies ... that we will think eternal ... Lord, that we will not have a shortsightedness ... that we will realize that every gift that You give to us is grace. That we could live out our life, Lord, only by You, for apart from You, we're nothing. We need all of Your strength and all of Your grace each and every moment of our lives.*

We ask for this, Lord, in the coming year. Let us be a light and a witness for the world out there that is unbelieving, that mocks God. There is more concern with what they want, with their own self-righteousness than with the righteousness of God. Father, we ask all of these things in Jesus' name. Amen.

A few hours after Pete uttered that prayer, he was in his eternal home. After years of hearing people cheering them, Pete and Press had to wrestle with some of the darkest issues of life resulting in their heartache and complete silence from the crowd. When they heard the cheering for the last time, they both felt empty. But, because both men discovered the answer as to why their lives mattered, this story of great American sports heroes ends on the most positive of notes.

"We are citizens of heaven, Darrel," Pete boldly pronounced to me. "Can you wrap your mind around that? I wouldn't trade that for all the money in the world. No awards, no accolades, and no material possessions. Nothing. I don't want people to remember me for anything else I've done; not for what I did on the basketball court; not for making it into the Hall of Fame. None of that."

"Sum up for me what people should remember about Pete Maravich," I requested.

"I want everyone to remember that all my life I searched everywhere for happiness, but when I found Jesus Christ, happiness found me. End of story."

THE END

28771864R00171

Made in the USA
San Bernardino, CA
08 March 2019